Introduction to the

Criminal Justice Process

Introduction to the
Criminal Justice Process

Published 1995 by
WATERSIDE PRESS
Domum Road
Winchester SO23 9NN
Telephone or Fax 01962 855567

ISBN Paperback 1 872870 09 0

Cover design by John Good Holbrook Ltd, Coventry

Printing and binding by Antony Rowe Ltd, Chippenham

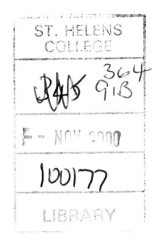

Introduction to the

Criminal Justice Process

Bryan Gibson and Paul Cavadino

WINCHESTER

Introduction to the
Criminal Justice Process

CONTENTS

Foreword

The criminal justice process encompasses all the procedures and practices which flow from the detection and apprehension of offenders. It embraces police dealings with suspects; the charging, cautioning and prosecution of offenders; bail and remand decisions; pleas, trials and sentencing; and arrangements for carrying out custodial and non-custodial sentences. An understanding of the criminal justice process as a whole requires a knowledge of how people are dealt with and how decisions are made at each of these stages.

In this book, we have sought to describe the different aspects of the process in a manner which will leave the reader with a clear understanding of its overall structure. Our aim has been to avoid excessive complexity but to provide a full enough description to enable the reader to grasp all the main features of the process.

We hope that the result will be of value not only to the student or lay person seeking an overall account of the subject, but also to the practitioner who wishes to have an improved understanding of the wider context in which his or her work takes place.

Bryan Gibson
Paul Cavadino

July 1995

Introduction to the
Criminal Justice Process

The authors

Bryan Gibson is a barrister, author and a former justices' clerk. His career has included three years as co-editor of *Justice of the Peace* and seven years as Chairman of the Criminal Law Committee of the Justices' Clerks' Society. He is a director of Criminal Justice Associates.

Paul Cavadino is Chair of the Penal Affairs Consortium, an alliance of 26 organizations concerned with the penal system, and Clerk to the Parliamentary All-party Penal Affairs Group.

Part I

The Criminal Courts

CHAPTER 1

Overview

No-one ever paused to devise a blueprint for criminal justice in England and Wales. This is one reason for the title of this book—what exists is a 'process' of justice, a network of closely linked organizations, each with its own separate role, objectives, working practices and history.

Some parts of this process are quite ancient in origin, such as the magistrates' court, High Court and the appellate jurisdiction of the House of Lords—see the chapters which follow—whilst others have been created at different times such as police forces in the Victorian era, the probation service at the turn of this century and the Crown Court and the Crown Prosecution Service (CPS) by statutes passed as recently as 1971 and 1985 respectively. The disparate nature of criminal justice began to diminish following Lord Woolf's report into prison disturbances (1991) which led to the creation of a national Criminal Justice Consultative Council and corresponding area committees comprising leaders of the different organizations (commonly called 'agencies') involved in the criminal justice process. The thinking permeates at local level via court 'user groups'—whilst issues like liaison, partnership and 'working together' have been high on the agenda. But it remains the case that there is nothing in the nature of a Ministry of Justice, or a truly co-ordinated approach.

NATURE OF THE PROCESS

One reason for these divisions is the doctrine of the separation of powers—the notion that the Legislature (Parliament), Executive (the Government) and Judiciary (the Courts) should be independent of each other. In the context of criminal justice, this means eg that the government or Home Secretary can, with Parliament's independent and democratic agreement, legislate about law and order but that neither Parliament nor ministers of the Crown can dictate to the courts what a particular law means or how it should be applied to a given case.

In the case of judges and magistrates this is known as 'judicial independence'. The courts have a long tradition of independent

9

decision-making—of freedom from improper influence or 'back door' information. They apply the law according to the facts of each case, subject only to control by other courts in the hierarchy on appeal. Likewise, each of the other participants such as the police, Crown Prosecution Service, probation service and prison governors have working cultures where independent decision-making is the norm.

Ultimately, this acts as a considerable restraint on the abuse of power or political oppression. There are thus strengths in a process in which the constituent parts—some of which operate closer to the interests of the state, or are more susceptible to influence from the centre than others—function independently. But it can also produce weaknesses.

Thus, for example, there is no co-ordination of the use of resources. A decision by a court to impose a particular sentence takes no account of the existence or otherwise of resources (but see now under the heading *Costs of criminal justice*, below). The diversion of an offender away from the formal criminal justice process, or from prison into a community based sentence, does not mean that the relatively high cost of bringing a case to court or of a bed in prison can be transferred to some other use. Nor do resources or facilities follow young offenders dealt with by local authorities instead of in young offender institutions, or a mental patient (a substantial proportion of offenders suffer from some form of mental disorder) who is treated in hospital rather than prosecuted. In the past, the autonomous nature of the criminal justice agencies enabled practices to develop which were quite insupportable—geared to the aims and objectives of the individual organization, arrived at unilaterally and often driven by working practices which resulted in an 'easy life' or greater financial return for members of that organization. Thus, acceptance of the idea that the agencies, whilst independent of one another, are 'interdependent'— which has occurred in the 1990s—represents a considerable advance.

An 'interdependent' process

The underlying rationale of interdependence is that each of the constituent parts of the process are to some extent reliant on each other in providing effective arrangements. In a sense, all criminal justice organizations bear joint responsibility for making the network of arrangements work. In this, the courts represent a focal point for the participating organizations and those individuals caught up in the process of justice.

The trend is for all concerned to work towards better information, good communications and improved performance—with standards of good practice a high priority *within* each organization. A common device is the court user group at both Crown Court and magistrates' court level, which meets to consider items of common concern and to develop good working practices. Similar exchanges take place at national level with a view to creating best practice, agreeing targets (eg for the time taken to reach each stage in court proceedings), and establishing sound operational methods.

THE NATURE OF CRIMINAL JUSTICE

Criminal justice is a topic which spans the criminal law, criminal procedure, the sentencing of offenders and the framework of organizations and procedures within which these aspects of the law of England and Wales operate. To an extent, the topic also touches on the thinking which underpins these arrangements.

Again, nowhere is there to be found a definitive statement of the purposes of criminal justice—although for a brief period following the implementation of the Criminal Justice Act 1991 and before parts of that Act were changed in 1993 it seemed that the purpose of a central aspect of criminal justice—sentencing—was fairly well established (see *Chapter 9*). Similarly, criminologists and practitioners may debate about the rationale, purpose or utility of an individual aspect of the topic. It is thus not always possible in this book to explain why a rule or practice exists as opposed to describing it as it is.

A main purpose in having a criminal justice process at all is to try and ensure 'law and order' as it is often termed. Methods have varied over the years, just as different criminal justice procedures exist in different countries of the world—ranging from liberal to draconian regimes. A distinct feature of the approach in England and Wales has been that attempts to control criminal behaviour have generally involved local responsibility as opposed to central provision or intervention.

The present arrangements can be divided as between the system of criminal courts and the other participating agencies. The scheme of this book is to describe:

* the system of criminal courts (Part I)
* the chronological progress of a criminal case from the time when an offence is first detected up until the end of a possible prison sentence and the supervision of the offender in the community which will generally follow this (Part II); and

11

- the key actors in this process (Part III).

Finally, the book examines what, in effect, are a number of independent issues such as the recommendations of the Royal Commission on Criminal Justice, the existence of a strong impetus to ensure that victims are considered at every stage, and measures aimed at removing discrimination from decision-making.

STRATEGIC MANAGEMENT

Just as there is no 'Ministry of Justice', neither is there a minister or other overall director of the various strands in the criminal justice process. At the highest level, there is a balance of functions as between the Lord Chancellor and the Home Secretary—broadly speaking resulting in a division between responsibility for the judiciary and criminal justice policy respectively.

Role of the Lord Chancellor

The Lord Chancellor is appointed by the Queen on the recommendation of the Prime Minister. Quite uniquely under the British constitution, the role requires that the occupant plays a part in all three arms of state (see above). He or she is a senior member of the cabinet, speaker of the House of Lords and head of the judiciary—and sometimes performs this last function by sitting in the House of Lords as a Lord of Appeal. A main task of the Lord Chancellor is to ensure the efficient *administration* of justice and of the courts. (The post also carries responsibility for promoting reforms in certain aspects of the *civil* as opposed to the criminal law).

The Lord Chancellor is responsible for the selection and appointment, or recommendation for appointment, of virtually all judges, judicial officers and magistrates in England and Wales (and also in Northern Ireland). He or she has general responsibility for the Court of Appeal, the High Court, the Crown Courts and the magistrates' courts—and for the county courts and administrative tribunals. All courts except magistrates' courts are now administered through an agency of the Lord Chancellor's Department called the 'Court Service'. Responsibility for the framework within which the magistrates' courts operate, and for the training of magistrates extends to the whole of England and Wales except Lancashire, Greater Manchester and Merseyside, where, for historical reasons, magistrates are appointed by the Chancellor of the Duchy of Lancaster.

The Lord Chancellor also has responsibility for the appointment of Queen's Counsel (QCs), ie usually barristers, who thereby progress to the rank of leading counsel: see generally *Chapter 12*.

Parliamentary secretary

In 1992, a junior minister with the title 'Parliamentary Secretary' was appointed to the Lord Chancellor's Department to represent that department in the House of Commons.

The Lord Chancellor's Department

The Lord Chancellor's Department (often referred to as 'the LCD') has been in existence for over 900 years. In its current form, the department—which employs some 9,000 people—is responsible to the Lord Chancellor for the administration of justice in England and Wales, working to '. . . support the Lord Chancellor in his task of administering the court system'. In the context of criminal justice this includes eg oversight of the Crown Court, swearing in juries, oversight of the locally administered magistrates' courts and strategic planning for court services.

The department has an annual expenditure of over £795 million (1993/1994) for the administration of justice and over £1.3 billion for the provision of legal aid, the scheme for the payment out of public funds of the legal costs of those who meet the appropriate eligibility criteria (see *Chapter 12*).

The Home Secretary

The Home Secretary is responsible for criminal justice policy and criminal law reform—as opposed to matters affecting judicial decision-making or the running of the courts. He or she also occupies a key role in relation to policing, prisons and the probation service as well as having quite separate responsibilities in relation to immigration and deportation.

The Home Secretary is currently assisted by four junior ministers—three ministers of state and a Parliamentary under-secretary of state. The division of responsibility between them alters from time to time. In July 1995 one minister of state was responsible for the police, crime prevention, criminal policy, partnership and drugs; another was responsible for probation, throughcare and the voluntary sector; while the third was responsible for prisons, life-sentences and mentally disordered offenders. The Parliamentary under-secretary of state was responsible for extradition and miscarriages of justice.

The Home Office

The Home Secretary is supported by the Home Office which, in particular, develops and implements relevant new criminal justice legislation, including the creation and updating of offences, procedure, and the framework within which sentences are imposed by the courts. These functions are accompanied by a substantial programme of research. Each year the Home Office publishes the *Criminal Statistics* showing the numbers of offences committed and sentences imposed.

The Home Office has a Criminal Policy Department with responsibility for the following:

- criminal law (offences, bail, procedures and sentencing)
- co-ordination within the criminal justice process
- alleged wrongful convictions
- mentally disordered offenders
- support for victims
- criminal injuries compensation
- international co-operation
- juvenile offenders
- Royal Commission on Criminal Justice.

It also has a Police Department and a Criminal Justice and Constitutional Department, whose responsibilities include the probation service. The Prison Service is an executive agency headed by a Director General who is responsible to the Home Secretary: *see Chapter 14.*

THE CRIMINAL COURTS

The criminal courts of England and Wales are:

- magistrates' courts: *Chapter 2*
- the Crown Court: *Chapter 3*
- the High Court, Court of Appeal and House of Lords: *Chapter 4;* and
- the youth court (a part of the magistrates' court with special responsibility for people below the age of 18 years): *Chapter 5.*

There are also Courts Martial (ie military courts to deal with service personnel), but these play a somewhat specialised role and are not dealt with in this book.

OTHER CRIMINAL JUSTICE ORGANIZATIONS

Apart from the criminal courts of law, the other main participants in the criminal justice process are as follows:

- the police as preventors, detectors and investigators of crime and who are responsible for initiating most prosecutions. Many police forces now have an 'administration of justice' department' to deal with court process, or the more traditional 'bench office'. Other key individuals are local custody officers and gaolers: *Chapters 6* and *11*

- the law officers of the Crown: *Chapter 12*

- the Crown Prosecution Service (CPS) which is responsible for most prosecution decisions once a case has been started. This includes reviewing the evidence to see whether a case is worth pursuing, deciding on the appropriate charge—and making decisions primarily on the basis of an 'evidential test' and 'in the public interest'. The CPS can take over, discontinue or withdraw proceedings (and it must assume responsibility for police prosecutions): see generally *Chapters 7* and *12*

- other regular law enforcement agencies including; the Serious Fraud Office (SFO); Customs and Excise; Department of Social Security; the Health and Safety Executive; 'Trading Standards'; the TV Licence Records Office; the NSPCC and RSPCA: *Chapter 11*

- legal representatives, ie solicitors and barristers: *Chapter 12*

- the probation service which provides a range of services to the courts. Probation officers observe 'National Standards for the Supervision of Offenders in the Community', including a standard for the preparation of pre-sentence reports (or PSRs)—written assessments of offenders and their offending which courts consider before sentencing in many cases. Probation officers are 'officers of the court' but work separately from it and independently. Probation facilities, or those arranged by the probation service, enable courts to use community sentences, eg 'probation centres', probation hostels, and community service projects—and conditional bail eg requiring residence in a hostel until the case comes back to court. Probation officers also work inside prisons as part of throughcare and 'sentence planning': *Chapters 8, 9* and *13*

• youth justice units (YJUs) which comprise social workers and probation officers and have a comparable function to the probation service but in relation to people under 18 years of age: *Chapter 5*

• local authorities who (apart from bringing civil care proceedings in respect of children and having responsibility for vulnerable adults) have a number of prosecution functions, eg the enforcement of bye-laws, consumer protection legislation and school attendance: *Chapter 13*

• prison governors, prison officers and prisoner escort services who deal with prisoners and provide transport for them to and from court (some tasks nowadays being discharged by the private sector): *Chapters 9* and *14*

• doctors and psychiatrists who are called upon to provide reports on the physical or mental condition of an offender or alleged offender from time to time: *Chapter 13*

• the non-statutory or voluntary sectors which provide a range of ancillary services to courts: *Chapter 13*

OTHER PARTICIPANTS

In addition to the above the court will be particularly concerned with the interests of:

• defendants in criminal cases (including ensuring that minority groups are not marginalised by court practices)
• witnesses (increasingly courts produce witness leaflets and provide 'witness care'): *Chapter 12*
• victims of crime (not directly involved in proceedings, except as witnesses, but whose interests should always be to the fore): *Chapter 18*

16

• the press and the public: see later in this chapter under the heading *Open court.*

Membership organizations
There is a range of membership organisations working in or around the criminal justice process which pursue policies that impact on the formal arrangements. These are noted in *Appendix I.*

GENERAL CONSIDERATIONS

There are certain general considerations which arise in relation to a criminal case and which can be dealt with conveniently at the outset. Some of these relate to the way in which the process of justice operates, others to the way in which cases are dealt with.

Open court
Members of the public are entitled to observe court proceedings, subject to there being available space and no interference. In exceptional circumstances, judges and magistrates can sit *in camera* (ie completely in private), eg in the interests of national security; or where life and limb is genuinely at stake—albeit that this is a fairly rare occurrence. Another situation is where there is evidence which—although it is not used by the prosecution—must be disclosed and it is claimed that the information is sensitive due to the way in which it was obtained (eg a police under-cover operation) or affects national security. The court may then decide that the correct course is to deal with the question of disclosure in private and even, in extreme instances, without the sensitive material being made known to the defendant or his or her legal representatives at all.

A common situation where a hearing is held in private is when a court is considering whether to issue a warrant of further detention during a police investigation under the Police and Criminal Evidence Act 1984 (PACE) although in such a case the suspect will usually be present: *Chapter 6.*

Youth courts are *not* open to the general public though the press can attend (but see below).

Photographing, drawing or tape-recording proceedings is punishable as a contempt of court—but a court can give leave for the use of a tape-recorder eg to an advocate who wishes to record complex evidence for transcription. The Crown Court takes its own shorthand note, however, which an advocate might be expected to rely on.

Press restrictions

Seats are normally reserved for the press in court and representatives are entitled to be present except in those rare instances when proceedings are held *in camera*, above.

The press can report what they will of proceedings except in a very few situations where an Act of Parliament restricts this, or allows the court to do so, eg transfer proceedings (where only a bare outline of the case can be reported unless the defence applies for restrictions to be lifted): *Chapter 3*; or where publication is postponed by order of the court to avoid a 'substantial risk of prejudice to the administration of justice'. Other legal restrictions on what can be reported exist in relation to the youth court, children (where the court makes what is called a 'section 39 direction') and a limited range of other matters.

The presumption of innocence

It is almost trite to state that in England and Wales an accused person is presumed innocent unless and until proved guilty—following the decision of a jury or magistrates. The presumption affects the way in which people are dealt with at all stages of the process.

Burden and standard of proof

The burden is on the prosecutor in a criminal case to establish the allegation to the required standard of proof—beyond reasonable doubt.

Just occasionally the law reverses the normal onus of proof and the defendant must establish something eg where this is exclusively within his or her own knowledge or that he or she held a licence or was covered by insurance—things that it is virtually impossible to prove otherwise. The standard of proof in these exceptional instances where the defendant has to prove something is always the lesser 'balance of probabilities'.

The right to silence

For many years it has been a feature of criminal justice in this country that an accused person enjoys a right to remain silent. But whereas in the past that was the end of the matter, the principle being that the prosecutor must prove all aspects of the case without resort to the fact that an accused person declined to give an explanation, since 1995 it is possible for inferences to be drawn where the right is exercised before or at the trial.

Trial by peers

Trial in the Crown Court by a jury of ordinary people selected at random (*Chapter 3*), or by lay magistrates (*Chapter 2*), is sometimes described as 'trial by peers', ie the principle is that people accused of crime are, so far as the question 'Guilty or not guilty?' is concerned, dealt with by members of the community, not by the state or a professional judiciary. The one exception to the latter is a small corpus of stipendiary magistrates (ie salaried magistrates).

Due process

There is no great principle of 'due process' in England and Wales in the sense that there is eg in the United States of America—but nonetheless the requirements are such that people can only be interviewed, arrested, tried and sentenced if the correct procedures are followed at each stage. In most instances, a material failure to follow correct procedure will prevent a conviction or constitute grounds for an appeal—unless, eg it is possible to deal with the case without resort to evidence or other item affected by the irregularity.

The three categories of offence

All criminal cases—whether unlawful parking or murder—start out in the magistrates' court. This may be by way of information and summons or arrest and charge, as explained in *Chapter 8*. But a distinction must be drawn between allegations which magistrates can actually try (ie decide upon guilt or innocence, then pass sentence) and those where they can only deal with the preliminary stages in order to see whether the case should be transferred to the Crown Court for trial on indictment.

There are, in effect, three categories of offence:

- summary
- 'either way'; and
- indictable only.

Summary offences

In the normal course of events, summary offences can *only* be tried— and, if convicted, the offender can *only* be sentenced—by magistrates. Everyday examples of summary offences (sometimes called 'purely summary' or 'summary only') are:

- speeding and other road traffic offences such as careless driving, defective brakes, lights or steering, driving with excess alcohol in the blood or urine, and taking a vehicle without consent
- no television licence
- lesser public order offences
- common assault
- criminal damage—depending on the value of the damage (currently below £5,000)
- certain social security offences
- being drunk and disorderly
- offences against local bye-laws.

Most summary offences are dealt with by summoning the alleged offender to court. Many cases take just a few minutes in court—if the defendant pleads guilty. Lesser offences are often dealt with by way of a written plea of guilty (subject to the appropriate procedures being invoked by the prosecutor: see under the heading *Paperwork cases* in *Chapter 8*). A plea of 'not guilty' attracts all the protections, rights and procedures of the criminal law. The trial of a purely summary offence must eg observe the same general rules as a trial for the most serious of matters.

The penalties for summary offences are laid down in the Act of Parliament which creates the offence. In practice, the maximum penalty is often a fine although some of the more serious summary offences can result in imprisonment.

Either way offences
The next level of offence is styled 'triable either way'—often referred to simply as an 'either way' offence. This means that the case can be tried either in the magistrates' court or in the Crown Court. The choice depends on the outcome of a procedure known as mode of trial (sometimes called 'choice of venue', or 'determining venue'). This is noted in *Chapter 8*.

Common examples of either way offences are:

- theft
- handling stolen property
- deception
- burglary (unless 'aggravated', eg with a firearm or weapon)
- criminal damage where the value is £5,000 or more
- assault occasioning actual bodily harm (abh)
- possession or supply of certain prescribed drugs.

Indictable only offences

'Indictable only' offences *must* be tried in the Crown Court before a judge and jury. Preparations to transfer the case to the Crown Court for trial begin immediately and the only question for the magistrates is whether there is sufficient evidence: *Chapter 3*. Examples of indictable only offences are:

- murder and other homicides
- rape
- robbery
- aggravated burglary (eg with a weapon)
- serious firearms offences
- conspiracy by two or more people to commit a criminal offence.

Legally speaking, the umbrella classification 'indictable offence' includes both indictable only and either way matters—hence the need for the terms 'indictable *only*' and 'either way' to distinguish cases which must or may be transferred to the Crown Court respectively.

Reasons for decisions

The general rule is that the criminal courts do not have to give reasons for their decisions (although they must have valid reasons and these are often explained in practice). There is an obligation to give reasons by law in some situations, eg:

- if not awarding compensation
- when sending someone to prison
- when not activating a suspended sentence
- when refusing bail or granting conditional bail.

These special cases are mentioned in appropriate chapters.

Crime, recorded crime and reported crime

There is a difference between the amount of crime which actually occurs (something which it is impossible to establish with any certainty), crime reported to the police and crime which is recorded in compliance with standard requirements. The amount of crime which survives the entire process from commission to an eventual sentence is sometimes put as low as two per cent of all crime (or three per cent if police cautions are also counted).

Discrimination

Section 95 Criminal Justice Act 1991 requires the Home Secretary to publish each year:

> ... such information as he considers expedient for the purposes of ... facilitating the performance by [persons engaged in the administration of criminal justice] of their duty to avoid discriminating against any person on the ground of race, sex or any other improper ground.

Several Home Office publications have been issued as a result of this provision starting with *Race and Criminal Justice* (1992): see Chapter 16 and, for a more detailed account, *Criminal Justice in Transition* (Waterside Press, 1994).

The costs of criminal justice

Similarly, since 1992, the Home Secretary has been under a duty to publish details of the costs of criminal justice. It should, however, be stressed that cost is not a factor in decision making, except, perhaps, to the extent that this is consistent with prior considerations affecting the interests of justice.

Criminal law and procedure

The law affecting a given topic is contained principally in Acts of Parliament, and in Rules and Regulations—known as Statutory Instruments (SIs)—in the common law and in the rulings of the higher courts (as reported in authenticated law reports). Practice Directions are also issued from time to time, usually, in relation to criminal procedures, by the Lord Chief Justice.

Law reports

Where a point is a difficult one—or argued in depth by the lawyers in the case—it may be necessary to refer to the full report of a ruling of the higher courts and to consider the comments of the Judges when giving their rulings.

Such reports—known as 'law reports'—are authenticated by a barrister and may sometimes be loosely referred to as 'precedents' (since that is what a ruling establishes). Law reports in regular use in the criminal courts include: the *All England Law Reports; Weekly Law Reports; Criminal Appeal Reports* (a special series of which deals exclusively with sentencing); *Justice of the Peace Reports;* and *Road Traffic Reports.* Practitioners also keep abreast of developments via short law reports which appear daily in *The Times* and other broadsheet newspapers.

CHAPTER 2

Magistrates' Courts

For the most part, magistrates' courts are served by ordinary members of the public who sit on the bench two or three times each month as a form of public service. Magistrates, or 'justices of the peace' (terms normally interchangeable), are chosen by the Lord Chancellor for their character, integrity and judgment. They are *lay* magistrates, ie not trained or skilled in the law—and not paid, other than their expenses plus a modest allowance if earnings are lost by attending court. They are advised by qualified lawyers: justices' clerks and their support staff. This approach accords with the basic principle that the law is made and enforced on behalf of the people and, in this respect, the arrangement is not dissimilar to that in the Crown Court (see *Chapter 3*) where 12 ordinary members of the public—the jury—determine guilt or innocence. However, in addition to the 30,000 or so lay justices there are towards 100 stipendiary magistrates, ie salaried professionals who are empowered to sit alone.

SUMMARY JUSTICE

Magistrates' courts are often described as courts of 'summary jurisdiction', a term which connotes the idea of a quick and inexpensive response to crime—the provision of fairly immediate remedies for minor offending. For the greater part this is the case, and summary justice proceeds at a relatively fast pace compared with the business of other courts, and even in some instances in the absence of the offender. Many lesser cases involve little more than transgressions as opposed to crimes in the full sense of the word and some of these take only minutes to deal with (particularly where paperwork procedures are adopted in respect of written pleas of guilty: *Chapter 8*). However, magistrates do deal with many matters which are both serious, complex and of considerable import: see under the heading *Jurisdiction*, below.

Justices of the Peace
The description 'justice of the peace' first appeared in the fourteenth century, although its origins can be traced back to the 'keepers of the peace' appointed by Simon de Montfort in 1264. The Justices of the

Peace Act 1361 built upon emerging powers to arrest suspects and investigate offences. Three or four of '. . . the most worthy in each county' were commissioned to dispense justice locally. Powers to punish offenders were added before the end of that century

Property qualifications were abolished in 1905 in favour of seeking out people with the personal qualities and suitability for the role. The bench has become broad based, more representative of the community that it serves and it is more balanced than in earlier years as between social background, age and gender (although there is still a considerable way to go in some parts of the country). Further information about the modern-day magistrate is contained in *Chapter 12*.

Justices' clerks and the management of magistrates' courts
The system of summary justice relies for its effectiveness on the unique nature of the relationship between justices and their advisors. The chief legal advisors to magistrates are the justices' clerks. Everyday advice in court is provided by one of a team of court clerks or 'legal advisors' (the more modern description). The advisor is not party to the decision of the court and legal rules dictate when he or she should intervene, or enter the magistrates' retiring room.

For many years, the justices' clerk was also the manager of the court—and this may well continue to be the position in practice in large parts of the country—but since the Police and Magistrates Courts Act 1994, each magistrates' courts committee must appoint a justices' chief executive to take overall responsibility for the day-to-day administration of courts in its area, so that the precise arrangements now depend on how that Act has been implemented locally.

An outline of the respective roles of justices' clerks, justices' chief executives and magistrates' courts committees—including the critical separation of 'legal or judicial' and 'administrative' functions—is contained in *Chapter 12*.

JURISDICTION

The word 'jurisdiction' is used to describe the extent of authority to deal with cases. In the criminal context, magistrates' courts have a wide range of responsibilities, including:

- dealing with around 98 per cent of all prosecuted crime in England and Wales, from start to finish—the remainder being sent by magistrates to the Crown Court for trial or sentence.

Virtually all criminal cases begin in the magistrates' court, even though some cases (eg murder, rape and robbery) *must* later go to the Crown Court: *Chapter 3*
- deciding whether an accused person is guilty or not: *Chapter 8*
- sentencing offenders (with powers of up to six months' imprisonment for a single offence in many instances or 12 months in total where sentences for two or more either way offences are imposed to run consecutively). The full range of court sentences is set out in *Chapter 9*
- authorising further detention under the Police and Criminal Evidence Act 1984 (PACE): *Chapter 6*
- deciding whether an offender ought to be released on bail or be kept in custody whilst awaiting trial: *Chapter 8*
- dealing with people aged under 18 in a special youth court: *Chapter 5*
- dealing with applications affecting property seized by the police and over which there may some a dispute concerning possession or ownership
- issuing warrants of arrest or to search premises
- discharging a range of administrative duties, either at court or in some instances 'at home'.

LOCAL JUSTICE

Magistrates' courts are essentially local courts. They deal principally with matters arising in their own area. The workload varies with the make-up of the area. There are around 600 court centres in England and Wales, serving cities, towns and rural areas. A busy city court is likely to see a greater proportion of serious crime (or 'heavy crime') than a remote rural area; a 'motorway court' will see a high percentage of road traffic cases; ports and airports generate Customs and Excise prosecutions; country areas witness agricultural crimes and poaching. Where the court is large enough, different kinds of cases may be streamed eg into 'remand courts', 'traffic courts', 'not guilty cases', 'non-police courts' and so on, whereas the daily list (or agenda) in a smaller court may contain all these varieties of case and more.

Petty sessional divisions
The unit of operation of the magistrates' court is the 'petty sessional division', or 'PSD'. The largest PSDs are in places like Birmingham, Liverpool and Manchester, with over 500 magistrates each. At the

opposite extreme, there are small benches (some with less than a dozen magistrates) although the trend is for these to combine to form a single, larger PSD with one bench chairman, one courthouse and so on. Alternatively, several PSDs may be grouped together within a single administrative unit, ie under one justices' clerk. Each bench then retains its identity, but there are shared arrangements for legal advice and support services.

Bench chairmen and deputy chairmen

Each PSD—or local bench—has a bench chairman whose role it is to oversee the general affairs of the bench, as well as to chair the court when present. The chairman is influential in shaping bench policy (eg the local starting points for sentences for particular offences; the preferred ways of conducting court proceedings). He or she will also act as a sounding board for the views of members of the bench—who as ordinary members of the community are exposed to every shade of public opinion and concern.

A secret ballot for the post of chairman takes place at the bench Annual General Meeting in October—when the successful candidate must obtain more than 50 per cent of the votes cast. The term of office is one year from the following January 1. If re-elected, the same individual may serve up to a maximum of five one-year terms. Local practice can mean that eg a voluntary three year rule is observed.

A bench will have one or more deputy chairmen (sometimes called vice-chairmen) who are appointed in a similar way, but without there being any requirement to obtain a given percentage of the votes cast.

The PSD can, if it so wishes, adopt a statutory nominations procedure in relation to the appointment of the chairman and deputy chairmen. In the event that '. . . the number of nominations does not exceed the number of offices available those nominated shall be declared elected'. Otherwise there is a secret ballot.

Presiding justices

For some years, many PSDs have appointed what they term 'court chairmen' or 'day chairmen'. A busy court centre may have a dozen or more courts running every day and all needing someone other than the bench chairman or one of the elected deputy chairmen to preside. From the beginning of 1996, only magistrates whose names appear on a list of approved court chairmen are eligible to act as a 'presiding justice' (except under supervision for training purposes). The list is drawn up by a chairmanship committee which, in turn, is appointed by the bench. Similarly, from 1996, no-one can preside unless they have undertaken a course of instruction under arrangements approved by the Lord Chancellor.

HEARINGS BEFORE MAGISTRATES

By far the general picture across the country is one of lay magistrates sitting to hear cases, but with stipendiaries sitting additionally in London and other urban centres.

Sittings of lay magistrates

Lay magistrates normally sit 'in threes' (the legal maximum) to decide the outcome of cases, but a court is properly constituted provided that at least two justices are present. (Some functions can be discharged by a single justice—below; and special rules apply to youth courts: *Chapter 5)*. In terms of significance the core functions of magistrates are:

- to decide whether someone should be granted bail or be held in custody pending the next stage in the proceedings
- to decide on guilt or innocence when a defendant pleads 'not guilty'
- to decide on the appropriate sentence where someone stands convicted, including, in serious cases, whether or not the offender should lose his or her liberty.

These tasks are hedged about with the other responsibilities already mentioned above—whilst magistrates who belong to specialist panels (there is a family proceedings panel in addition to the youth court panel) have extra, equally demanding duties.

Evidence, argument and representations

Magistrates listen to evidence and argument, sometimes called 'representations' or 'speeches'. They might then adjourn, ie leave the courtroom to discuss matters in their private retiring room. If legal advice is required, they can call upon their legal advisor for this part of the discussion. Once they have arrived at a decision it is announced in court by the chairman. A short explanation may sometimes be added. There is an obligation to give reasons by law in those situations already mentioned in *Chapter 1* as well eg as when a decision is made not to endorse someone's driving licence or not to impose a mandatory driving ban in respect of a road traffic offence.

Straightforward cases are often dealt with without adjourning. The chairman consults on the bench and gives the decision of the court there and then. A complex case might need to be considered for a significant period of time in the privacy of the magistrates' retiring room—whereas a simple case might be resolved in minutes.

Decisions by a single justice
Some decisions can be taken by a single magistrate. An example is whether to allow bail or to place an alleged offender in custody pending the hearing of the case (ie a 'remand': *Chapter 8*). Saturday 'stand by' courts often have just one magistrate. Cases might then be put over to Monday morning to be dealt with by a 'full court'. A range of 'out of court' duties can be carried out by a single justice: *Chapter 2*.

Stipendiary magistrates
As well as lay magistrates, there are towards 100 stipendiary magistrates, or 'stipes'. They are paid professional lawyers and are empowered to act alone. They are located mostly in London and the larger urban centres—although stipendiaries have also been appointed to serve some counties on a shared basis, as between several PSDs. A stipendiary can be called in by any bench, eg at times of abnormal pressure, or to deal with a special or locally sensitive case.

Stipendiary magistrates have all the powers of a lay bench. They tend to work speedily by comparison—being trained professionals, and with no need to retire to consult. However, the Lord Chancellor has confirmed that there is no question of wholesale replacement of the lay magistracy by professionals.

NATURAL JUSTICE

The rules of natural justice are of acute importance in magistrates' courts due to the close involvement of lay magistrates in their own local communities. The twin pillars of natural justice can be stated as

- no-one can be a judge their own cause; and
- always hear both sides.

The rule against bias
Courts must always be impartial. The rule that no-one can be a judge in their own cause is sometimes called 'the rule against bias'. If bias does exist the magistrate concerned is disqualified from sitting to hear the

case—except when bias can properly be waived by the parties. A magistrate who has a *financial* interest in the outcome of a case must not sit; and neither should he or she do so if there is a close personal relationship or other interest—such as a connection with one of the parties or a witness, or there is a business or career association. Remote interests can be 'waived' with the agreement of the parties—provided the interests in question are disclosed and no pressure is applied to get the parties to forgo their right to object. Financial interest can never be waived. The rule against bias extends to appearances. But there must be a real danger of bias before a justice is disqualified or the court becomes tainted with it.

Hear both sides
The other requirement of natural justice is that each party must be given a full and proper opportunity to put their case. This aspect of the rule is sometimes put by saying that the court must act fairly. Again, it extends to appearances. Decisions have been quashed by the High Court on appeal eg where a magistrate 'dozed off' (or appeared to do so); or made some injudicious remark.

CONTEMPT OF COURT

Magistrates have power to punish for contempt of court. This extends to anyone who wilfully insults the court or a justice, or any witness, officer of the court or lawyers—in all cases either in court or whilst going to or returning from court. The same applies where anyone wilfully interrupts proceedings or misbehaves in court. Offenders can be detained until the end of the proceedings and, if the court thinks fit, committed to custody for up to a month or fined up to £2,500 (July 1995), or both. A committal to custody can be revoked at any time, eg where the offender asks to apologise (thereby showing contrition and 'purging' the contempt).

CHAPTER 3

The Crown Court

The Crown Court sits at over 90 locations across England and Wales. It replaced the former Assizes and Quarter Sessions in 1974 following a comprehensive review by Lord Beeching which led to the Courts Act 1971. Sometimes, courtrooms are situated in prestigious, often grand civic buildings eg in the major cities or county towns—but equally, nowadays, Crown Court premises are modern, functional, anonymous in appearance and cost-effective. Even where the 'Number 1 Court' sits in impressive surroundings, overspill accommodation for other courts can be quite Spartan.

The court is usually named after its location, eg Liverpool Crown Court, Leeds Crown Court, Winchester Crown Court—although each will deal with cases from a wider catchment area. Strictly speaking, they all part of 'the Crown Court'—ie a single institution operating nation-wide—and each venue a 'Crown Court centre'. The Central Criminal Court (or 'Old Bailey') is part of the Crown Court and deals with cases arising in central London and those transferred to it from other parts of the country for reasons eg of local sensitivity, security or convenience to the parties and witnesses. It is a regular feature for cases to be transferred between all Crown Court centres in the interests of justice and effectiveness.

JURISDICTION

In general terms, the Crown Court deals with serious offences, the two to three per cent of prosecuted crime which filters beyond the magistrates' court. There are several strands to its criminal jurisdiction:

- the trial of criminal cases before a judge and a jury, ie involving

   —very serious offences which are triable only on indictment such as murder, manslaughter, rape, robbery (*Chapter 1*)
   —either way matters where the magistrates' court has declined jurisdiction or the accused person has elected trial by jury (*Chapter 1*)

30

—summary matters which can properly be dealt with at the same time as either of the above

—allegations of 'grave crimes' made against people below the age of 18 where these must be committed to the Crown Court for trial or in those discretionary situations where the youth court has declined jurisdiction (*Chapter 5* and below)

• committals for sentence by magistrates' courts in respect of either way offences
• appeals against conviction or sentence by magistrates, or against both of these. Such convictions may be in respect of summary or either way matters (see generally *Chapter 10*).

In terms of the place where an offence is alleged to have been committed, the jurisdiction of the Crown Court extends across England and Wales. The court can also deal with offences committed in territorial waters, on British ships and with treason or the murder of a British subject wherever allegedly committed.

TRANSFER FOR TRIAL AT THE CROWN COURT

The process by which cases reach the Crown Court is known as transfer for trial. Where an offence is indictable only—or the magistrates' court has determined that trial at the Crown Court is more appropriate or the defendant has elected for trial by jury in respect of an either way offence—the proceedings before the magistrates turn into 'transfer proceedings', ie proceedings with a view to transfer for trial at the Crown Court.

Transfer proceedings were about to be brought into force as this book was being written. Until they are—and during a short transitional phase—the relevant procedure is known as 'committal for trial' and magistrates carry out the functions of 'examining justices' to see whether there is a case for committal. However, forms of transfer proceedings have existed in relation to cases involving serious fraud and offences against children for some years. Ever since 1967, there has been a general power to conduct a 'paperwork committal' without consideration of the evidence.

Transfer for trial represents a significant development in that, whilst it is dealt with 'on the papers', the magistrates' court has nonetheless to consider the evidence. This is contained in a file of documents known as the 'notice of the prosecution case'. In practice, written statements of witnesses are likely to form the bulk of the case (there is no provision at the transfer stage for the calling of 'live' witnesses, something which must wait until any Crown Court hearing). The magistrates must also consider any written representations from the defendant contained in an 'application to dismiss'. If there is sufficient evidence to justify the transfer then the case is transferred for trial. Transfer may be on the charge already put to the accused or on any amended or substituted charge disclosed by the evidence. Only if the court permits it—in a complex or difficult case—are there any oral representations at the transfer stage (except where the defendant is unrepresented, when he or she is entitled to make representations in person). Otherwise, everything happens 'on the papers'.

The magistrates then decide whether the defendant should be allowed bail or be held in custody pending his or her arraignment before a judge and jury (below). In due course, the accused will be required to answer to the indictment (below). If he or she is allowed bail but fails to appear at the Crown Court, a 'bench warrant' will be issued by that court—which may be with or without bail.

VOLUNTARY BILLS OF INDICTMENT

It is possible for cases to start out in the Crown Court rather than in the magistrates' court—by way of what is called a voluntary bill of indictment, ie where a written application, supported by other documentation, is made direct to a High Court judge who may order a trial in the Crown Court. In cases where magistrates have refused to transfer a case to the Crown Court this is the only route which remains open to the prosecutor if he or she wishes to pursue the matter.

JUDGE AND JURY

The business of the Crown Court is arranged according to the upper level of seriousness of criminal offences with which a particular centre deals and, correspondingly, the level of judge who normally presides at that centre. The most serious cases are dealt with by a 'first tier' Crown Court and usually before a High Court judge. The vast bulk of offences—second and third tier matters—are dealt with by a circuit judge or a recorder. Descriptions of the personnel concerned are contained in *Chapter 12*.

All trials take place before a judge and a jury of 12 ordinary members of the public empanelled at random for each and every case where a plea of 'not guilty' is entered (although the same jury may deal with several cases in succession where these are short and heard over a relatively brief timespan).

Trial by jury is sometimes described as 'trial by peers' (something said to be guaranteed by Magna Carta). Given that a criminal trial may involve complex issues of law or fact, this method of doing justice through the deliberations of inexperienced lay people is achieved via a careful separating out of the functions of the judge and the jury:

• The judge has general charge of the course of the trial and deals with all matters of a legal nature, such as purely technical submissions or legal argument (usually in the absence of the jury so that they are not tainted by knowledge of items which may not become part of the evidence in the case). He or she is responsible for ruling on the admissibility of evidence, and on practice and procedure—and also for deciding certain questions of mixed fact and law such as whether the jury should hear about an alleged confession said to have been made by the accused person but which it is now claimed was obtained by duress or oppression, or whether other evidence should be ruled out as prejudicial. The judge must withdraw a case from the jury if there is insufficient evidence to support a conviction.

Before the start of a case, the judge is responsible for items of a preliminary nature and may make orders concerning the progress of the case—sometimes known as 'practice directions'. At the conclusion of a jury trial, the judge is responsible for summing up to the jury, ie reminding them of the evidence and directing them as to its possible effect. In the event of a conviction, the judge passes sentence—often after considering a pre-sentence report (PSR).

• The jury decides whether the accused is guilty or not guilty, in effect by considering all factual matters which are relevant to whether the accused committed the offence for which he or she has been indicted. Subject to procedural safeguards, the judge can accept a majority verdict (below) and a jury can return an 'alternative verdict': see *Chapter 8*. Jury deliberations are confidential.

ARRAIGNMENT

The accused is 'arraigned' in the Crown Court (as opposed to being 'charged' before magistrates), ie the clerk of the court calls upon the accused by name, reads over the indictment (below) and asks whether he or she pleads 'guilty' or 'not guilty'.

THE INDICTMENT

'Indictment' is the name given to the formal document in which the allegation against an accused person is set out in writing. Indictments may contain several allegations, or 'counts' as they are known, but an individual count can only allege a single offence. Several people can be charged in the same indictment. These basic rules are supplemented by others affecting the circumstances in which offences or offenders can be tried alongside one another (known as 'joinder'). Applications may need be made to the judge before the case reaches the jury to settle these matters.

TRIAL

The accused is asked to plead to each of the counts in the indictment. The data indicate that many cases turn into guilty pleas once they have been transferred for trial. Every attempt is made by the Crown Court to expedite cases, but in some areas of the country it is still possible to spend a long period on remand awaiting trial. If a plea of 'not guilty' is entered, the trial follows the general pattern outlined in *Chapter 8*.

VERDICT

The initial outcome of a criminal case is the verdict of 'guilty' or 'not guilty', again dealt with in *Chapter 8*. The basic rule is that the verdict of the jury must be unanimous. However, it is possible for the judge to accept a majority verdict provided that at least 10 of the twelve jurors are of the same mind. This can only occur after the jury has been allowed time (at least two hours, or longer in a complicated case) to arrive at a unanimous verdict, but the judge is satisfied that this cannot be achieved.

SENTENCING POWERS

The powers of the Crown Court range up to life imprisonment, which is mandatory for murder and discretionary for eg manslaughter and rape. Many of the more serious offences carry a maximum sentence of fourteen years in prison. Sentences may be made consecutive to one another or concurrent. The general principles which affect sentencing decisions and the range of sentences, orders and other options are outlined in *Chapter 9*.

APPEALS

Appeals from decisions of the Crown Court in criminal cases—against either conviction or sentence, or both—are heard by the Court of Appeal (Criminal Division). There is a further appeal to the House of Lords in certain circumstances: see *Chapter 10*.

PEOPLE UNDER 18 AND 'GRAVE CRIMES'

Generally speaking, people below the age of 18 who are accused of criminal offences are dealt with in the youth court: *Chapter 5*. However, it is possible for such defendants to reach either the magistrates' court or in some cases the Crown Court as a result of their being charged alongside an adult. Whilst such cases are in practice separated out wherever possible so that the defendant who is below the age of 18 is tried or dealt with independently by the youth court, this is not always possible—and it may be that the interests of justice will require that both accused people are tried together, by the same court and at the same time.

Quite apart from this there are provisions whereby people below the age of 18 may be committed to the Crown Court for trial in respect of what are known as 'grave crimes': see *Chapter 5*.

RIGHTS OF AUDIENCE

In general terms, rights of audience (ie the right to address the court on behalf of a client) in the Crown Court are restricted to barristers (sometimes called 'counsel') and those solicitors in private practice who are licensed to practice in that court. Employed solicitors, such as members of the Crown Prosecution Service are not allowed to represent their employers so that, as a case progresses from the magistrates' court to the Crown Court, the conduct of that case must be handed over from the Crown Prosecution Service to a barrister where this has not already occurred. A move which would have allowed Crown prosecutors their own rights of audience foundered in 1995. Barristers retained by the Crown are known as 'Treasury counsel'. Senior barristers or 'Queen's Counsel' (QCs) appear in the more serious cases. The Courts and Legal Services Act 1990 enabled a wider range of people to acquire rights of audience in the Crown Court—either generally or in a given case. A general note about barristers and solicitors is contained in *Chapter 12.*

CROWN COURT CIRCUITS

For administrative purposes the Crown Court is divided into a number of 'circuits' serving different regions of the country. These are the Midlands and Oxford circuit (based on Birmingham); Northern circuit (Manchester); North Eastern circuit (Leeds); South Eastern circuit (London); Wales and Chester circuit (Cardiff); and the Western circuit (Bristol).

ADMINISTRATORS AND CHIEF CLERKS

Each Crown Court circuit is headed by an administrator and each Crown Court by a chief clerk. The chief clerk is responsible among other things for the management of the Crown Court centre, listing and scheduling of cases, the calling and swearing-in of jurors and the care of witnesses (subject in the case of items affecting judicial matters to the direction of the judge). In court, a member of his or her staff acts as a court clerk, calling on cases, swearing in jurors and witnesses, putting the indictment to the accused and generally dealing with day-to-day matters affecting the course of a given case. Unlike the position in the magistrates' court, the court clerk is not a qualified lawyer and does not perform advisory, legal or judicial functions in relation to the trial. These are a matter for the judge. There are however some functions performed by clerks in the Crown Court which are of a quasi-judicial nature, such as the taxing of bills of costs submitted by a party following an award of costs by the judge.

THE CROWN COURT USER GROUP

As in the magistrates' court, there is a 'user group' in the Crown Court made up of regular participants in the criminal justice process. The membership reflects the different priorities of that court. It is often chaired by a circuit judge and will eg include members of the Crown Court administration and representatives of the Bar as well as the usual agencies: police, Crown Prosecution Service, Law Society (ie solicitors), magistrates' courts, the probation and prison services. Such groups function alongside and in addition to 'Area Criminal Justice Liaison Committees'—the regional tier of the national Criminal Justice Consultative Council.

CONTEMPT

The Crown Court has wide powers to punish for contempt of court including dealing with cases of contempt before magistrates which have been committed to it for sentence.

CHAPTER 4

High Court, Court of Appeal and House of Lords

For the far greater part, criminal cases end with conviction and sentence, or acquittal, in either the magistrates' court or Crown Court as described in the last two chapters. However, there are various routes by which a case may go to appeal beyond these courts—to the High Court, Court of Appeal and House of Lords. Avenues of appeal are dealt with in *Chapter 12* in accordance with the chronological scheme of that part of this book. These higher courts have no 'first instance' jurisdiction except the House of Lords in the case of a peer of the realm who may opt to be tried by the House, ie by his or her peers. In modern times, members of the House accused of criminal offences have invariably opted to be tried by the ordinary courts.

HIGH COURT

The High Court deals principally with the more important civil disputes and is split into three divisions: the Queen's Bench Division, Chancery Division and the Family Division. It is centred in London at the Royal Courts of Justice in The Strand (often referred to by practitioners simply as 'The Strand'), but may also sit in selected towns throughout England and Wales.

In terms of criminal matters, the Queen's Bench Division of the High Court is the most significant division. It is presided over by the Lord Chief Justice and, although it has a broad remit to deal with civil actions for damages arising eg from breach of contract and libel, commercial disputes and Admiralty cases, a 'Divisional Court' of the Queen's Bench Division deals with appeals from magistrates' courts and Crown Courts by way of case stated.

Additionally, the High Court has a general supervisory function over a wide range of courts, tribunals and bodies or individuals performing public functions—including the criminal courts and government ministers. This function of 'judicial review' is mainly to ensure that decisions made by these bodies or individuals do not go beyond the powers given by Parliament.

COURT OF APPEAL

As its name implies, the Court of Appeal deals exclusively with cases on appeal. It has no first instance jurisdiction. The court comprises two divisions, criminal and civil. It is again housed in the Royal Courts of Justice in The Strand. Both divisions may refer cases involving points of law to the House of Lords.

- *Criminal Division*

The Criminal Division hears appeals from people convicted in the Crown Court and its senior judge is the Lord Chief Justice, who is responsible for the way the court is run and is likely to set the tone of the court and its stance towards the criminal law during his or her period of office. The history of the centrally important office of Lord Chief Justice is ably described by Anthony Mockler in *Lions Under the Throne* (Muller, 1983). Leave is required before there can be an appeal: see *Chapter 12.*

- *Civil Division*

In contrast, the Civil Division of the Court of Appeal is headed by the Master of the Rolls and hears appeals from the High Court and county courts.

The chief significance of the Court of Appeal (Criminal Division) for the criminal justice process is that it gives rulings—judicial guidance on sentencing—which inform, and in some instances liberate or constrain, the sentencing practices of the Crown Court and magistrates' courts. Key rulings become known as 'guideline judgments': see *Chapter 12.* A judge of the Court of Appeal is called 'Lord Justice'.

HOUSE OF LORDS

Appeals to the House of Lords are heard by the Appellate Committee of the House which is presided over by the Lord Chancellor (who sometimes sits as a judge in that court) and is the final court of appeal in the United Kingdom for both criminal and civil cases from England and

Wales. Leave is required before there can be an appeal: see *Chapter 12*. Scottish criminal cases have no right of appeal there.

The Appellate Committee of the House is made up of Law Lords (otherwise called Lords of Appeal in Ordinary), who are life peers. They never number more than 11 and are either former holders of high judicial office or former practising barristers of at least 15 years' standing who are appointed to carry out the judicial function of that House. The Committee sits apart from the main business of the House of Lords and there is a convention that Law Lords do not engage in political debate—except where this is of direct judicial concern. Law Lords were, eg active in the debates which led to the Police and Magistrates' Courts Act 1994 (which is now the principal statute governing administration of the magistrates' courts) and helped to secure a number of changes to the original proposals.

Rulings of the House of Lords—the judgments of the Law Lords are known as 'speeches'—are of considerable import in relation to the day-to-day proceedings of the lower courts and have almost the same impact as legislation. Thus, eg when in 1995 the House of Lords had to deal with the question whether the ancient rule of *doli incapax* should be abolished (whereby the law requires that a person under the age of 14 must—over and above the other ingredients of an offence—be proved to have known that what he or she was doing was 'seriously wrong'), the House, whilst acknowledging the need for a review of the law, declined to alter matters. Such a fundamental change was something more appropriately dealt with by Parliament itself. However, there have been instances where what the House has decided has, in effect, altered the way in which courts applied the criminal law (eg marital rape has been held to be a crime where it was not so regarded previously). It is, seemingly, still open to the House to create, or at least to rediscover, common law criminal offences.

Privy Council

A judicial committee of the Privy Council (in effect the Appellate Committee in another guise, but possibly supplemented by foreign judges) sits as a final court of appeal from some Dominion territories, or former territories who have opted to continue with this last avenue of appeal as an adjunct to their own appeals system. Rulings are 'persuasive' (ie rather than binding) so far as the courts of England and Wales are concerned.

CHAPTER 5

The Youth Court

The investigation, processing and outcome of cases involving people below 18 years of age follows a similar pattern to that in relation to adults, subject to additional safeguards, procedures and sentencing powers. Thus eg there are special provisions in the PACE Codes of Practice for investigating officers, including a duty to ensure that someone concerned with the welfare of the person is informed and to secure the involvement of an 'appropriate adult' (see *Chapter 6*).

DIVERSION FROM THE COURT PROCESS

For some years now, efforts have been made to divert young people away from court whenever appropriate. Whilst this approach has come under scrutiny, the objective is nowadays achieved by:

- informal warnings; and
- official police cautions—sometimes linked with other strategies which are designed to avoid court proceedings (and often known as 'caution plus' schemes).

There may be a 'youth bureau', or 'youth panel' (not to be confused with the youth court panel already mentioned)—which operates on a day-to-day basis to advise the police on decisions on whether to initiate the prosecution of people below the age of 18.

When prosecution *is* necessary, the conventional wisdom involves recognising that many young people pass through a difficult stage in their lives and are apt to challenge or test out authority. Sometimes this brings them into conflict with the criminal law. For the most part, courts try to avoid the more severe forms of punishment unless they consider that these are unavoidable.

SPECIAL ARRANGEMENTS

The youth court was established in 1992 to replace the former juvenile court, created in 1908. The single most important change was to bring

41

17-year-olds within the new jurisdiction—thereby, correspondingly, increasing the minimum age for the adult court from 17 to 18 years of age. The youth court deals almost exclusively with *criminal* cases (certain *civil* functions affecting the care of young people who may not be in trouble with the criminal law having been removed to the family proceedings court by the Children Act 1989: see *Chapter 7*).

The youth court functions under the administrative umbrella of the magistrates' court and subject to the same general laws—which are then overlaid with a variety of special powers and procedures.

THE YOUTH COURT PANEL

Youth court magistrates belong to a statutory 'youth court panel' and receive special training which emphasises the differences between offending by adults and young people—often at a transitional stage in their lives. Except in London where youth court magistrates are appointed direct to the panel, they also continue to serve in the adult court. The panel appoints its own chairman and deputy chairmen; and meets eg for training purposes and to keep in touch with developments, local sentencing facilities, and youth justice practice.

CHILDREN AND YOUNG PERSONS

The youth court deals with 'children' and 'young persons':

- 'children' are aged 10 to 13 years inclusive
- 'young persons' are aged 14 to 17 years inclusive.

The word 'juvenile' continues to be used by many practitioners to describe people dealt with by the youth court. Children and young persons will normally appear and be sentenced in that court although they can appear in the adult magistrates' court eg for the purposes of remand when no youth court is sitting, or if charged jointly with an adult. If they are convicted in the magistrates' court, that court has some powers to sentence them but these are limited to a discharge, fine, parental bind over or a supervision order. Offenders under 18 years of age are normally remitted to the youth court for sentence—and must be remitted except where one of these options is in mind.

There is no mode of trial procedure in the youth court in the ordinary sense (see *Chapter 3*) but there *is* power to commit young persons to the Crown Court for sentence. Also, a youth court can decline, at the outset, to deal with some very serious offences and must do so in certain instances. Thus, the youth court has no power to deal with cases of homicide (murder, manslaughter etc), which must be sent to the Crown Court for trial, whilst other allegations—in respect of 'grave crimes' such as rape, wounding, aggravated burglary or sexual assaults—can, according to the nature of the offence and the age of the offender, be sent to that court for trial and a possible sentence under section 53 Children and Young Persons Act 1933.

REMANDS

As with adults, children and young persons can be granted or refused bail and subject to the same basic procedures: see *Chapter 9*. But whereas defendants aged 17 and over (NB *not* '18 and over': there is an anomaly in relation to remands) who are remanded in custody go to a prison or a remand centre, a refusal of bail to someone below that age operates as a remand to local authority accommodation. Where a defendant *is* remanded to local authority accommodation, the authority can seek permission from the court to use secure accommodation. Where a young person is 15 or 16 and *male*, the court can remand him in custody if strict statutory criteria are satisfied. Further detail is beyond the scope of this introductory work but can be found in *Bail: The Law, Best Practice and the Debate* (Waterside Press, 1993).

THE WELFARE PRINCIPLE

The youth court represents one of the more enlightened aspects of criminal justice. There is a history of creative sentencing and of extra care to avoid unsuitable punishments. Much of this stems from the welfare principle contained in section 44 Children and Young Persons Act 1933 and which operates in all courts (and whether eg the person concerned appears as a defendant or as a witness):

> Every court in dealing with a child or young person who is brought before it either as an offender or otherwise shall have regard to the welfare of the child or young person.

This principle has to be reconciled with the 'just deserts' sentencing philosophy introduced by the Criminal Justice Act 1991, the principles of which apply equally to offenders below the age of 18 as they do to adults.

PARENTAL RESPONSIBILITY

The relevant statutory provisions place great stress on parental responsibility, particularly in relation to younger offenders—but that responsibility starts to diminish with the onset of maturity. Thus, the white paper *Crime, Justice and Protecting the Public* (1990) argued that:

> . . . Young people should begin to take more responsibility for the consequences of their own decisions and actions. They are at an intermediate stage between childhood and adulthood. The arrangements for dealing with offenders [aged 16 and 17] should reflect this.

Conversely, the white paper argued that parents might be expected to exercise greater control over younger children and to accept some responsibility for their actions, including paying for their misbehaviour.

The procedural and sentencing arrangements reflect this. Courts *may* require the parents or guardians of 16-year-olds and 17-year-olds to attend court and to pay financial penalties imposed on their child. Similarly, the court *may* bind over the parents or guardians of offenders aged 16 and 17 to take proper care of and to exercise proper control over the offender. They can also bind over the parent or guardian to ensure that the young person complies with the requirements of a community sentence. However, the court is not placed under a duty to exercise these powers as it is in relation to offenders below the age of 16.

With these younger offenders the court *must* exercise its powers to require parents or guardians to attend court or to pay any financial penalty imposed unless the parents or guardians cannot be found or it would be unreasonable to do so—and, similarly, it must bind over the parent or guardian if it is satisfied that this would be desirable in the interests of preventing further offending.

CONSTITUTION

A youth court sitting must include both a man and a woman unless this is impracticable—and there is a minimum requirement of three justices (as opposed to two in the adult court). Youth courts are not open to the public. The press are admitted, but it is an offence to publish the identity of a juvenile unless the court specifically authorises this in an individual case to avoid injustice.

YOUTH JUSTICE SERVICES

The key agencies are social services and the probation service, often acting together in the shape of a youth justice unit (YJU, sometimes called 'integrated services') which concentrates on work with young offenders and writing expert pre-sentence reports: see next section. In many areas of the country there are multi-agency policy groups via which strategies are devised for keeping young people out of court and out of custody: see under the heading *Diversion*, above.

Pre-sentence reports
Reports on children and young persons are a specialist task, not least because there is normally a family involvement, but one which is apt to be fragile in many instances (often these offenders come from broken homes or disturbed backgrounds). Where the offender is still at school, relevant information may often be available from teachers and this will either be incorporated in the pre-sentence report (PSR) or be received by the court in the form of a free-standing school report. A PSR can only be dispensed with before passing a custodial sentence or the more intensive community sentences on an offender under 18 if there is an earlier report which the court can consider. However, good practice in relation to people in this age group—whose lives and circumstances can change rapidly—means that a fresh report *is* usually obtained.

SENTENCE

In outline, the sentencing powers of the youth court are as follows:

- *absolute or conditional discharge*

- *fines and compensation orders*
The general criteria for fines apply to children and young persons subject to overall cash limits, ie £250 in the case of a child; £1,000 for young persons. Parents or guardians who are ordered to pay the fines of their children—see *Parental responsibility* above—are assessed on the basis of their own means, not those of the child.

45

• *community sentences*

Two community sentences—supervision orders and attendance centre orders—are available for young offenders aged 10 years or over. In addition, probation orders, community service orders, combination orders and curfew orders are available for those aged 16 or over. Except for supervision orders, these are explained in *Chapter 9* in relation to offenders aged 18 or over.

Supervision orders may be made for up to three years. The supervisor will be a local authority social worker or a probation officer. The order may include requirements for the child or young person:

—to live at a particular place
—to attend at a specified place at specified times
—to take part in various forms of activity (including, in some instances, highly intensive programmes of supervised activities)
—to remain at home for specified periods between 6pm and 6am
—to refrain from taking part in specified activities
—to receive psychiatric treatment
—to attend school or follow other educational arrangements
—to live in local authority accommodation for a specified period of up to six months.

• *custody*

Young people aged 15 or over can be sentenced to detention in a young offender institution run by the prison service. The minimum sentence is two months and the maximum two years for 15 to 17 year olds. When the relevant provisions of the Criminal Justice and Public Order Act 1994 are in force, 12 to 14-year-olds will be eligible for a secure training order, to be served in one of five secure training centres managed by private sector organizations on behalf of the Home Office. Long term detention for 'grave crimes' can be ordered by the Crown Court if the youth court sends the case there at the outset.

A comprehensive account of youth court practices and sentencing powers can be found in *The Youth Court One Year Onwards* (Waterside Press, 1993).

Part II

Due Process

CHAPTER 6

Investigation, Arrest and Charge

The criminal justice process begins when a crime is reported, but formal action can only be taken when the process of detection and investigation leads to the identification of a suspect and ultimately to someone being charged with an offence.

DETECTION

Crimes may be detected in a wide range of ways including:

- information from the victim or other members of the public
- offenders being caught in the act.
- admissions by suspects during questioning (ie a 'confession')
- the analysis of forensic and circumstantial evidence.

Some crimes are cleared up when an offender who is charged with or convicted of an offence admits to a number of other offences. Sometimes these offences are taken into consideration when sentence is passed (known as TICs: see *Chapter 9*).

An offence is said to be 'cleared up' where:

- a person has been charged or a summons issued
- a person has been cautioned
- the offence is admitted and could be taken into consideration

or, in some cases where no further action is taken, if there is sufficient evidence but the case is not proceeded with eg because it is admitted in a prison interview with a person already serving a custodial sentence for another offence, because the offender is under the age of criminal responsibility or because the victim is unable to give evidence.

The clear up rate, or detection rate, is the ratio of offences cleared up in a year to offences recorded in a year. Overall, 25 per cent of recorded crimes are cleared up; but for violent and sexual offences the clear up rates are much higher, at 76 per cent and 75 per cent respectively. Some offences have better clear-up rates because there is a high likelihood of the victim being able to identify the offender eg many sexual offences, or knowledge of the offence may directly identify the offender as in the case of handling stolen goods, going equipped for stealing and trafficking in controlled drugs.

THE COURSE OF AN INVESTIGATION

An investigation into a criminal offence may involve interviewing many prospective witnesses and assembling other evidence of the kind described in *Chapter 8*, such as exhibits, forensic reports and expert opinion. Relevant information must only be obtained by acting within the law and special legal provisions come into play as soon as there is a suspect—breach of which may result in evidence being ruled inadmissible by a court.

Arrest, search and seizure
The police enjoy wide powers of arrest and search in respect of people suspected of criminal offences either under the general law or in relation to particular kinds of offence. Similarly, the police have power to take possession of property where they believe it to be the subject of a criminal offence (such as stolen goods or a prohibited drug), to have been used or intended for use in committing an offence (such as a weapon, tool, key, vehicle, account book or forgery), or where an item might become evidence. Procedures exist through the magistrates' court concerning the return of property where ownership is later in dispute, whilst the courts have power eg to order restitution or compensation to a victim of crime: see *Chapter 9*.

In many instances, the police require a warrant from a magistrate in order to search eg for stolen goods or drugs—but powers exist to seize property where the police are already lawfully on premises or where the level of seriousness of an offence justifies an immediate response such as an emergency entry. Where a warrant *is* required, the application must be made on oath and must normally be authorised by a senior officer before being made.

Arrestable offences and serious arrestable offences
Certain offences are arrestable by definition—irrespective of any free-standing power to arrest in relation to a particular offence—ie principally those which attract a maximum sentence of imprisonment of five years or more. Where offences *are* 'arrestable' other powers go hand in hand with this fact.

Various powers rest on the investigation or charge being in respect of a 'serious arrestable offence'. This term applies first to certain offences listed in the Police and Criminal Evidence Act 1984 (known as 'PACE') which are always serious. In addition, any other arrestable offence may be regarded as serious if its commission has led, or is intended or likely to lead, to: serious harm to the state or to public order; serious interference with the administration of justice or the investigation of offences; the death of, or serious injury to, any person; and substantial financial gain or loss to any person.

Bail by a police officer

An arrested person may be granted bail by a police officer during an investigation for re-appearance at a police station—or, after being charged with a criminal offence, for appearance before a magistrates' court at a fixed time. Since 1995, this can be conditional bail and all references to police bail in this chapter must be construed in this context. The Bail Act 1976 obliges a police officer to make a record of any bail decision and, if requested to do so by the person in relation to whom the decision was taken, to provide a copy of this record. Where bail in criminal proceedings is granted by endorsing a warrant of arrest for bail the constable must also make a record: see generally *Chapter 8.*

PACE and the PACE Codes

Investigation and arrest fall within an array of legal provisions and approved practice created by PACE and the Codes of Practice made pursuant to that statute. There is provision throughout the PACE procedures for the individual concerned or his or her solicitor to make representations at appropriate times. PACE or the Codes have the following effects at key points in the process of investigation, arrest and charge:

Procedure on arrest

Where a person is arrested or taken into custody by a constable he or she must be taken to a police station as soon as reasonably practicable (except, of course, when already there). Certain statutory powers of arrest are exempted.

The station must be a 'designated police station' (below) if it appears that it may be necessary to keep the person in police detention for more than six hours—unless the constable will be unable to take the individual to a designated police station without injury and lacks the necessary assistance. Delay is authorised in certain instances. The person must be released if the constable becomes satisfied that there are no grounds for keeping him or her under arrest.

At the police station

If someone attends voluntarily at a police station or other place for the purpose of assisting the police with investigations or accompanies a constable without being arrested, he or she is entitled to leave at will unless arrested—when he or she must be informed at once of the arrest. Someone brought to a police station under arrest or who is arrested at the police station should be informed by the custody officer of the following rights and of the fact that they need not be exercised immediately:

- the right to consult the PACE Codes of Practice.

- the right to have someone informed of his or her arrest. A person arrested and held in custody is entitled on request to have a friend, relative or other person who is likely to take an interest in his or her welfare told, as soon as is practicable, that he or she has been arrested and is being detained. An officer of at least the rank of superintendent may authorise delay in the case of someone in police detention for a serious arrestable offence where he or she has reasonable grounds for believing that this will lead to interference with or harm to evidence concerned with such an offence, or interference with or physical injury to other persons, or that it will lead to the alerting of other suspects not yet arrested or hinder the recovery of property. Special provisions apply to terrorism offences.

- the right to consult a solicitor. A person arrested and held in custody in a police station or other premises is entitled on request to consult a solicitor privately at any time. Consultation must be permitted as soon as practicable except to the extent that delay is permitted. An officer of at least the rank of superintendent may authorise delay in the case of a serious arrestable offence if he or she has reasonable grounds for believing such consultation would have a comparable effect to that described in the last paragraph. The right is to consult privately, but an assistant chief constable or commander may authorise consultation to take place only in the sight and hearing of a qualified officer of the uniformed branch. Special provisions apply to terrorism offences.

Where someone is arrested without a warrant from a court but the custody officer at the police station to which he or she is taken considers that there is insufficient evidence to charge that person and is not prepared to hold that individual for questioning, or cannot legally do so, the custody officer must release him or her. But this may be on bail subject to a requirement to return to a police station at some later date.

Likewise, if a custody officer is conducting a review of detention (below) and he or she concludes that detention without charge can no longer be justified, the suspect must be released with or without bail.

After 24 hours
Similar decisions must be made at the end of 24 hours detention without charge. The basic rule is that a person must not be kept in police detention for more than 24 hours without being charged. This limit may be extended up to 36 hours by a senior police officer but only in the case of a 'serious arrestable offence'.

A police officer of the rank of superintendent or above who is responsible for the police station may authorise the keeping of a person in police detention for the period up to 36 hours if he or she has reasonable grounds for believing that:

- detention without charge is necessary to secure or preserve evidence or to obtain evidence by questioning the suspect;
- the offence is a serious arrestable offence; and
- the investigation is being conducted diligently and expeditiously.

When detention of a person of less than 36 hours is authorised a further period expiring not later than the end of the initial 36 hours may be authorised, provided the conditions are still satisfied.

Beyond 36 hours
Where continued detention *is* authorised by a senior officer, the detained person must still be released with or without bail at the expiry of 36 hours unless an application to a magistrates' court—sitting 'otherwise than in open court'—is made and results in a warrant of further detention being issued thereby allowing the police to continue to detain the suspect. Such warrants can be issued for up to 36 hours at a time, provided that the suspect is not detained for longer than 96 hours overall. He or she must then be released—although a fresh arrest is possible, but only if eg new evidence emerges.

51

Application must be made by a constable on oath, supported by information which must specify the offence, the general nature of the evidence on which the person has been arrested, what inquiries have been made and what further inquiries are proposed, plus the reasons for believing that continued detention is necessary. The court must be satisfied that there are reasonable grounds for believing that further detention is justified by virtue of the same criteria that govern the exercise of the superintendent's discretion: above. Application may only be made:

- before the expiry of 36 hours
- where it is not practicable for the magistrates' court to sit at the expiry of 36 hours but the court will sit during the six hours following the end of that period, before the expiry of those six hours.

This six hour period of leeway is not limited to the situation where the 36 hour period expires and no court is sitting at all. Justices also have a discretion during the course of a sitting whether to hear such an application straight away or to wait, provided they do so for no longer than six hours. The Code of Practice recognises the impracticability of a court's being convened outside the hours of 10 am and 9 pm.

Where not satisfied that further detention is justified it must refuse the application (but can adjourn within the basic, initial 36 hours). If the application is refused the arrested person must be charged forthwith or released with or without bail. However he or she need not be released before the expiry of 24 hours detention, or the expiry of any longer period for which continued detention has been authorised by a superintendent, ie up until the end of the initial 36 hours.

Where application is made after the expiry of 36 hours and it appears that it would have been reasonable for the police to have made the application in time, the court must dismiss the application.

After charge
Once someone has been charged with an offence at a police station, the police custody officer must decide whether to bail the accused for appearance at court or to arrange for him or her to be brought before a court within 24 hours for the court to take that decision.

If a person is charged with an offence the custody officer must order release from detention with or without bail unless one of a number of grounds is satisfied—eg that his or her name or address cannot be ascertained; that the custody officer has reasonable grounds for believing that the person will abscond, commit an offence or interfere with the administration of justice if released; or that detention is necessary for the person's own protection or, if a juvenile, in his or her own interests.

Anybody who, after being charged with an offence, *is* kept in police detention or detained by a local authority must be brought before a magistrates' court. If he or she is brought before a court for the petty sessions area in which the police station is situated this must be as soon as practicable and in any event not later than the first sitting after being charged with the offence. If no magistrates' court is due to sit on the day when he or she is charged, or the next day, the custody officer must inform the clerk to the justices who must arrange for a magistrates' court to sit within a brief statutory timescale.

Custody officers and their duties

Certain police stations must be designated by the chief officer of police to be used for detaining arrested people and one or more custody officers must be appointed for each designated police station. The custody officer must be of at least the rank of sergeant; but a non-involved officer of any rank may perform the function if a custody officer is not readily available.

It is the duty of the custody officer to ensure that all people in police detention are treated in accordance with PACE and the Codes of Practice. Special provisions cover the situation where an arrested person is taken to a police station which is not a designated police station, and to transfer between police stations.

Where someone is arrested for an offence or returns to a police station to answer to bail, the custody officer must, as soon as practicable, determine whether he or she has sufficient evidence to charge that person with the offence. If there is sufficient evidence, the suspect must be either charged or released without charge—with or without bail. Following a charge, the custody officer must order release either with or without bail of anyone arrested without a warrant other than in restricted circumstances set out in PACE.

Review of police detention

Periodic review of the circumstances of people in police detention must be carried out by the review officer who is, in the case of a person arrested and charged, the custody officer, and in the case of a person arrested but not charged, a non-involved officer of at least the rank of inspector. PACE sets out a timetable and the detained person or his or her solicitor is entitled to make representations at appropriate points.

Juveniles

If an arrested person is a juvenile, the custody officer must, if practicable, ascertain the identity of the person who is responsible for his or her welfare and inform that person that the juvenile has been arrested, and the reason why he or she is detained. If the juvenile is known to be subject to a supervision order, reasonable steps must be taken to notify the supervisor. The custody officer must also, as soon as practicable, inform an 'appropriate adult' of the grounds for detention and the juvenile's whereabouts and ask the adult to come to the police station to see the juvenile.

By 'appropriate adult' is meant the parent or guardian; or, if the juvenile is in care, the relevant care authority or voluntary organization; or a social worker; or, failing any of the above, a responsible adult who is not a police officer or police employee. The appropriate adult may or may not be a person responsible for the juvenile's welfare—and has an important role in advising and observing for fairness.

A custody officer who authorises an arrested juvenile to be kept in police custody must ensure that, after being charged, the arrested juvenile is moved to local authority accommodation unless he or she certifies either that it is impracticable to do so or, in the case of a juvenile aged 12 or over, that no secure accommodation is available and keeping the juvenile in other local authority accommodation would not be adequate to protect the public from serious harm from him or her.

Mentally handicapped and disordered suspects

Similar 'appropriate adult' procedures apply in relation to mentally handicapped and mentally disordered people.

CHAPTER 7

The Decision to Prosecute

Primarily, the decision to prosecute is one for the police (or other official organization charged with such a responsibility). The decision coincides with that to charge a suspect a described in *Chapter 6* or to 'lay an information' as outlined in *Chapter 8*. However, once proceedings have been started in this way, the decision whether a police prosecution should continue becomes one for the Crown Prosecution Service (CPS). In many instances, the CPS is consulted before proceedings are begun, particularly if some legal technicality is involved, the case is otherwise complex, or it involves someone below the age of 18 (see further at *Chapter 5*) or an especially vulnerable individual.

The Serious Fraud Office discharges a wider role in that within its field of operations it has both an investigative and a prosecution function—albeit that this may often be triggered by information provided by police forces.

CONSENTS

Certain offences can only be prosecuted with the consent or approval of the Director of Public Prosecutions (which can in practice be supplied by any Crown prosecutor) or the government's chief law officer, the Attorney General. The latter form of consent is often called a 'fiat'. These requirements do not prevent the investigation, detention and arrest of a person—or in most cases charging and remand.

CAUTIONING AND DIVERSION SCHEMES

The police have a discretion whether to charge an offender or formally to caution him or her. When an offender admits guilt and there is sufficient evidence for a conviction, the offender consents, and it is not necessary in the public interest to institute criminal proceedings, a caution may be given. A caution is a formal warning given by a senior police officer in uniform, normally at a police station.

Cautioning is governed by national standards, the most recent version of which was issued in 1994. Cautioning allows a range of less serious offenders a chance to reform without obtaining a criminal record. It is used particularly extensively for first time juvenile offenders who have committed minor offences. A caution can be an effective deterrent to offenders of all ages who have committed minor offences or who have offended for the first time. Most people who are cautioned do not reoffend: Home Office research shows that 85 per cent of those cautioned are not convicted of a 'standard list' offence within the next two years.

Home Office circulars in 1985 and 1990 encouraged greater use of cautions and the number of offenders dealt with in this way doubled during the last decade. However, following a change of government policy, a further circular was issued in March 1994 designed to reduce the number of cautions, in particular by discouraging the use of repeat cautions.

In some areas of the country inter-agency panels (typically including representatives of the police, social services, the probation service and the education or youth service) make recommendations to the police on whether cautioning of young offenders would be appropriate in individual cases. In appropriate cases such panels can make arrangements to refer young people and their families for advice, assistance or guidance in conjunction with a caution, and some arrange for mediation and reparation to victims in suitable cases. Such voluntary arrangements are often referred to as 'caution plus' schemes.

Cautions are subsequently cited in court if the offender commits a further offence for which he or she is prosecuted if the caution or cautions are relevant to the later offence.

CROWN PROSECUTION SERVICE

The Crown Prosecution Service is responsible for most public prosecutions in England and Wales and may take over any private or other prosecution. It has a duty to do so in relation to proceedings commenced by police forces—widely defined by statute. The governing provision is the Prosecution of Offences Act 1985, under which, among other things, the Director of Public Prosecutions (as head of the CPS) is under a duty to issue a Code for Crown prosecutors '. . . giving guidance on general principles to be applied by them.' The Code is explanatory of the day-to-day functions of the CPS, the processes of prosecution decision-making and its role within the criminal justice process. Descriptions of the personnel who make up the CPS and notes about its general running are contained in *Chapter 12*.

THE CODE FOR CROWN PROSECUTORS

The short form of the Code for Crown Prosecutors was last revised in June 1994. The Service also maintains a more detailed version for internal use and which, due largely to the sensitivity of some of the more intricate decisions which prosecutors have to make, is not available to the general public. The Code begins with a number of general statements and principles:

1. INTRODUCTION

1.1 The decision to prosecute an individual is a serious step. Fair and effective prosecution is essential to the maintenance of law and order. But even in a small case, a prosecution has serious implications for all involved—the victim, a witness and a defendant. The Crown Prosecution Service applies the Code for Crown Prosecutors so that it can make fair and consistent decisions about prosecutions.

1.2 The Code contains information that is important to police officers, to others who work in the criminal justice system and to the general public. It helps the Crown Prosecution Service to play its part in making sure that justice is done.

2. GENERAL PRINCIPLES

2.1 Each case is unique and must be considered on its own, but there are general principles that apply in all cases.

2.2 The duty of the Crown Prosecution Service is to make sure that the right person is prosecuted for the right offence and that all relevant facts are given to the court.

2.3 Crown prosecutors must be fair, independent and objective. They must not let their personal views or the ethnic or national origin, sex, religious beliefs, political views or sexual preference of the offender, victim or witness influence their decisions. They must also not be affected by improper or undue pressure from any source.

The continuing duty to review cases
In a civil case, the High Court has held that the CPS owes a duty of care to people who are subject to its decisions. The high standards

demanded by the duty to review cases and to make effective decisions as to whether a case should continue or not are encapsulated as follows:

3. REVIEW

3.1 Proceedings are usually started by the police. Sometimes they may consult the Crown Prosecution Service before charging a defendant. Each case that the police send to the Crown Prosecution Service is reviewed by a Crown prosecutor to make sure that it meets the tests set out in this Code. Crown Prosecutors may decide to continue with the original charges, to change the charges or sometimes to stop the proceedings.

3.2 Review, however, is a continuing process so that Crown prosecutors can take into account any change in circumstances. Wherever possible, they talk to the police first if they are thinking about changing the charges or stopping the proceedings. This gives the police the chance to provide more information that may affect the decision. The Crown Prosecution Service and the police work closely together to reach the right decision, but the final responsibility for the decision rests with the Crown Prosecution Service.

The twin tests

Crown prosecutors apply twin tests when reviewing a case, the 'evidential test' and the 'interests of justice' test. The first of these is sometimes explained by saying that for a prosecution to be launched or continued there must be a realistic prospect of conviction.

4. THE CODE TESTS

4.1 There are two stages in the decision to prosecute. The first stage is the evidential test. If the case does not pass the evidential test, it must not go ahead, no matter how important or serious it may be. If the case does pass the evidential test, Crown prosecutors must decide if a prosecution is needed in the public interest.

4.2 This second stage is the public interest test. The Crown Prosecution Service will only start or continue a prosecution when the case has passed both tests. The evidential test is explained in section 5 and the public interest test is explained in section 6.

5. THE EVIDENTIAL TEST

5.1 Crown prosecutors must be satisfied that there is enough evidence to provide a 'realistic prospect of conviction' against each defendant on each charge. They must consider what the defence case may be and how that is likely to affect the prosecution case.

5.2 A realistic prospect of conviction is an objective test. It means that a jury or bench of magistrates, properly directed in accordance with the law, is more likely than not to convict the defendant of the charge alleged.

5.3 When deciding whether there is enough evidence to prosecute, Crown prosecutors must consider whether the evidence can be used and is reliable. There will be many cases in which the evidence does not give any cause for concern. But there will also be cases in which the evidence may not be as strong as it first appears. Crown prosecutors must ask themselves the following questions:

Can the evidence be used in court?

(a) Is it likely that the evidence will be excluded by the court? There are certain legal rules which might mean that evidence which seems relevant cannot be given at a trial. For example, is it likely that the evidence will be excluded because of the way in which it was gathered or because of the rule against using hearsay as evidence? If so, is there enough other evidence for a realistic prospect of conviction?

Is the evidence reliable?

(b) It is likely that a confession is unreliable, for example, because of the defendant's age, intelligence or lack of understanding?
(c) Is the witness' background likely to weaken the prosecution case? For example, does the witness have any dubious motive that may affect his or her attitude to the case or a relevant previous conviction?
(d) If the identity of the defendant is likely to be questioned, is the evidence about this strong enough?

5.4 Crown prosecutors should not ignore evidence because they are not sure that it can be used or is reliable. But they should look closely at it when deciding if there is a realistic prospect of conviction.

6. THE PUBLIC INTEREST TEST

6.1 In 1951, Lord Shawcross, who was Attorney-General, made the classic statement on public interest, which has been supported by Attorneys-General ever since: 'It has never been the rule in this country—I hope it never will be—that suspected criminal offences must automatically be the subject of prosecution'. (House of Commons Debates, volume 483, column 681, 29 January 1951.)

6.2 The public interest must be considered in each case where there is enough evidence to provide a realistic prospect of conviction. In cases of any seriousness, a prosecution will usually take place unless there are public interest factors tending against the prosecution which clearly outweigh those tending in favour. Although there may be public interest factors against prosecution in a particular case, often the prosecution should go ahead and those factors should be put to the court for consideration when sentence is being passed.

6.3 Crown prosecutors must balance factors for and against prosecution carefully and fairly. Public interest factors that can affect the decision to prosecute usually depend on the seriousness of the offence or the circumstances of the offender. Some factors may increase the need to prosecute but others may suggest that another course of action would be better.

Common public interest factors

The Code goes on to list some common public interest factors, both for and against prosecution, explaining that these are not exhaustive and that the factors which do apply will depend on an individual case.

SOME COMMON PUBLIC INTEREST FACTORS IN FAVOUR OF PROSECUTION

6.4 The more serious the offence, the more likely it is that a prosecution will be needed in the public interest. A prosecution is likely to be needed if:

(a) a conviction is likely to result in a significant sentence;
(b) a weapon was used or violence was threatened during the commission of the offence;
(c) the offence was committed against a person serving the public (for example, a police or prison officer, or a nurse);
(d) the defendant was in a position of authority or trust;
(e) the evidence shows that the defendant was a ringleader or an organizer of the offence;
(f) there is evidence that the offence was premeditated;
(g) there is evidence that the offence was carried out by a group;
(h) the victim of the offence was vulnerable, has been put in considerable fear, or suffered personal attack, damage or disturbance;
(i) the offence was motivated by any form of discrimination against the victim's ethnic or national origin, sex, religious beliefs, political views or sexual preference;
(j) there is a marked difference between the actual or mental ages of the defendant and the victim, or if there is any element of corruption;
(k) the defendant's previous convictions or cautions are relevant to the present offence;
(l) the defendant is alleged to have committed the offence whilst under an order of the court;
(m) there are grounds for believing that the offence is likely to be continued or repeated, for example, by a history of recurring conduct; or
(n) the offence, although not serious in itself, is widespread in the area where it was committed.

SOME COMMON PUBLIC INTEREST FACTORS AGAINST PROSECUTION

6.5 A prosecution is less likely to be needed if:

(a) the court is likely to impose a very small or nominal penalty;
(b) the offence was committed as a result of a genuine mistake or misunderstanding (these factors must be balanced against the seriousness of the offence);
(c) the loss or harm can be described as minor and was the result of a single incident, particularly if it was caused by a misjudgment;
(d) there has been a long delay between the offence taking place and the date of the trial, unless:

- the offence is serious;
- the delay has been caused in part by the defendant;
- the offence has only recently come to light; or
- the complexity of the offence has meant that there has been a long investigation;

(e) a prosecution is likely to have a very bad effect on the victim's physical or mental health, always bearing in mind the seriousness of the offence;

(f) the defendant is elderly or is, or was at the time of the offence, suffering from significant mental or physical ill health, unless the offence is serious or there is a real possibility that it may be repeated. The Crown Prosecution Service, where necessary, applies Home Office guidelines about how to deal with mentally disordered offenders. Crown Prosecutors must balance the desirability of diverting a defendant who is suffering from significant mental or physical ill health with the need to safeguard the general public;

(g) the defendant has put right the loss or harm that was caused (but defendants must not avoid prosecution simply because they can pay compensation); or

(h) details may be made public that could harm sources of information, international relations or national security.

Balancing factors

The Code goes on to emphasise that deciding on the public interest is not simply a matter of adding up the number of factors on each side. Crown Prosecutors must decide how important each factor is in the circumstances of each case and go on to make an overall assessment, including the interests of the victim, '. . . which are an important factor, when deciding where the public interest lies'. It also gives advice on appropriate charges, mode of trial (see *Chapter 1*), the decision whether or not to accept a guilty plea to some but not all of the offences with which he or she is charged and the circumstances in which, occasionally, it is appropriate to re-start a prosecution after, eg it has been discontinued the first time around. Copies of the Code are available to the public by writing to: The Crown Prosecution Service, Information Branch, 50 Ludgate Hill, London EC4 7EX.

External opinions

The CPS is staffed and managed by lawyers, so that there is no want of legal expertise. However, it can sometimes occur that a case is very complex, or involves unusual technicalities or specialities, such that it is more expeditious or cost-effective for the CPS to obtain the opinion of counsel (ie a barrister) at the outset on whether the objectives set by the Code are met. Also, in some instances, counsel may be appointed at an early stage where the likely future course of the case indicates that the same advocate should remain in charge of the case throughout.

PRIVATE PROSECUTIONS

Except where it is expressly prohibited or where the consent or authority of some official is required by law, anyone can bring a 'private prosecution', ie commence criminal proceedings. Such an individual risks costs being awarded against him or her if the prosecution fails, or the attempt to lay an information being rejected as vexatious or an abuse of the process of the court, or the matter being taken over by the Crown Prosecution Service (and possibly its being discontinued by them after application of the tests already set out in this chapter). Nonetheless, a number of such prosecutions still occur each year, often in respect of quite serious offences, sometimes where the CPS has decided against prosecution—and occasionally, on the evidence of recent years, resulting in a conviction eg of someone charged with manslaughter, rape or serious offences involving the abuse of children. Whilst the costs of a successful private prosecution fall to be met from public funds, there is nothing in the nature of legal aid for this purpose.

Prosecutions by officials or official bodies other than the police are sometimes spoken of as 'private' or 'non-police' prosecutions. The wide range and individual nature of these is beyond the scope of this introductory work but *Chapter 11* contains a note of the main regular prosecutors other than the police.

CHAPTER 8

Bringing a Case to Court

Criminal proceedings are started either by laying an information or by arrest and charge. In practice, proceedings for most serious offences are started by this latter route. Following an investigation in accordance with the Police and Criminal Evidence Act 1984 (PACE), the defendant is charged by a custody sergeant and bailed to appear at court or, where appropriate, conveyed direct to court in custody: *Chapter 6*. The legal effect in terms of launching the case is the same. The individual who is accused will in due course be called upon to answer the allegation, unless eg it is discontinued by the Crown Prosecution Service in those cases where it has the conduct of a case and is therefore under a duty to review the evidence and consider whether prosecution is in the public interest: *Chapter 7*.

COMMENCING COURT PROCEEDINGS

Most court procedures are laid down by Act of Parliament, or in Statutory Instruments (also known as 'SIs', 'Regulations', 'Rules' or 'Rules of Court') drawn up by government ministers in consultation with interested parties and laid before Parliament.

Virtually all criminal proceedings start out in the magistrates' court and cases are then either dealt with to their conclusion by that court or are transferred to the Crown Court for trial (Chapter 3) or sentence (*Chapter 9*). Exceptionally proceedings may start in the Crown Court by way of a voluntary bill of indictment.

Information and summons
An information may be oral or written (although, increasingly, both are generated by computer input). In effect, it is an application for a summons (ie an instruction to attend court), and as such it must be laid before a magistrate or a justices' clerk. The decision whether to issue a summons is a judicial one—albeit that in practice vast numbers of run-of-the-mill summonses are issued every day with only minimal scrutiny unless there is some reason for caution.

A common situation in which oral informations occur is when the defendant is already present at court and the prosecutor wishes to alter the allegation. Another situation is where an ordinary member of the public makes an allegation, eg of assault by a neighbour, although this would be put into writing by court staff. Generally speaking, informations *are* in writing (computer input equating to this) and must be so where a warrant of arrest is applied for in place of a summons— when the information must also be substantiated on oath, something which can take place before a magistrate only.

An information is usually signed or validated by the informant but this is not strictly necessary. An information must contain the name of the informant, the name and address of the defendant, the allegation and enough details to indicate precisely what is being alleged ie the date, place and nature of the alleged offence and in practice the legal provision which makes it an offence.

Arrest and charge

The word 'charge' is often used quite loosely, to indicate any situation where an allegation is put to a defendant whether in court or by the police or other prosecutor. This loose meaning also covers the situation where an information is read out to the defendant in court, ie the court clerk might well say 'You are charged that . . . '. But when the word is used in its true sense, this is to make a distinction between proceedings by way of information and summons (above) and proceedings by way of arrest and charge as described in *Chapter 6*.

When the defendant is charged in this technical sense, a 'charge sheet' is completed, a copy handed to the defendant and another sent to the magistrates' court. No summons is issued—this is unnecessary as the defendant will have been released by the police on bail to appear at court or have been brought straight to court (usually within 24 hours, Sundays and Bank Holidays being excluded from this time limit).

Warrants of arrest

Warrants with or without instructions to bail the defendant to appear in court on a fixed date can be issued by magistrates, in a variety of situations:

- instead of a summons where the offence is imprisonable and a summons will not suffice (eg where the address of the alleged offender is unknown). The information must be in writing and substantiated on oath
- where the defendant has failed to answer a summons

- where he or she has failed to surrender to bail eg following being charged by the police and released on bail to attend court.

The Crown Court can issue a bench warrant eg where an accused fails to turn up for his or her trial. Failure to surrender to bail is known as 'absconding'. It is a basis for refusing bail in the future: see below. It can also be a criminal offence in its own right.

BAIL OR CUSTODY

Once charged, an offender must be released on bail or be brought before a magistrates' court in custody—usually within 24 hours.

Police bail
This may be for a suspect to return to the police station for an investigation to continue (*Chapter 6*) or for appearance at court following the defendant's being charged by the police—who now have power to grant bail with conditions attached: see below.

Court bail
The Bail Act 1976 guarantees a right to bail to people charged with a criminal offence, ie a right not to be held in custody unless one of several strict legal exceptions applies. If there *is* an exception, the defendant is remanded to a local prison, usually for not more than eight clear days at a time before conviction. Longer remands in custody are possible, in certain circumstances, for up to 28 days. After conviction, the limit on such a remand is 21 days.

More recent legislation has introduced important changes in that reasons now have to be given for granting bail in the case of murder and other prescribed offences; whilst bail cannot be granted at all in the case of a charge of murder or attempted murder, rape or attempted rape, or manslaughter if the defendant already has a conviction for one of these offences or culpable homicide. A new ground for refusing bail has also been created—an offender need not be granted bail if the offence is indictable (including either way matters) and the defendant was already on bail for an earlier offence when the later offence was allegedly committed. In another development, the prosecutor now has a right of appeal to the Crown Court against a grant of bail in certain cases (assuming that bail was opposed). The offence in question must be one punishable with imprisonment for five years or more or an offence of vehicle-taking.

Young people

People aged 17 to 20 who are refused bail are held in 'remand centres' or prisons. Below the age of 17, a refusal of bail operates as a remand to local authority accommodation. During such a remand period, the authority can seek permission from the court to use secure accommodation. Where the defendant is aged 15 or 16 and *male* the court can remand him to a remand centre or prison if strict statutory criteria are satisfied.

Refusal of bail—grounds and reasons

Apart from the exceptional cases described above, bail can only be refused if the court is satisfied that an exception to the general right to bail exists. Exceptions are known as 'grounds'. The court must state which ground or grounds exist and support these with valid reasons. Bail can be refused in relation to imprisonable offences before conviction if there are substantial grounds for believing that if given bail the defendant would:

- fail to surrender to custody (ie abscond)
- commit an offence
- interfere with witnesses.

The precise grounds vary according to whether or not the offence is imprisonable, and whether the decision is being made before or after conviction. The scope for refusing bail is less where the offence itself does not attract imprisonment. However, defendants can be held in custody for any offence for their own protection (eg to prevent attack) or where there has been a previous breach of bail by absconding and the court believes that the defendant would abscond if given bail again.

Repeat applications for bail

There are legal rules concerning repeat applications, ie the same arguments being put forward by defendants over and again at subsequent remand hearings. Courts are not obliged to listen to the same matters repeatedly. But this does not apply on a defendant's first two appearances.

Custody time limits

There are limits on the total length of time for which a defendant may be held in custody before a case starts. Either way cases tried by magistrates must be begun within 70 or 56 days (depending on whether mode of trial—*Chapter 3*—has been decided within the first 56 days, when the limit telescopes down to this shorter period). Where a case is to be transferred for trial, the transfer process must be started within 70 days. A period of 112 days is then allowed between the date when magistrates transfer the defendant to the Crown Court and arraignment (ie his or her appearance before a jury for the indictment to be read).

If a time limit expires, the defendant cannot be remanded in custody any longer. He or she may still be prosecuted, but must be released on bail (which may be 'conditional': see next section). However, time limits can be extended by the court for good cause.

Conditional bail
Bail can be granted with conditions, eg to live at a given address; report to the police '. . . between 6pm and 8pm every Monday, Wednesday and Friday'; not to associate with the victim or witnesses (a 'non-association' condition); or to stay away from a particular location. Reasons must be given for conditions. The police have power to grant conditional bail (except where this requires residence in a bail hostel and in a very few other instances). The defendant can be arrested for breach of a condition. Bail may then be revoked by the court. Unlike absconding, breach of a condition is not itself an offence.

Sureties and securities
A commonly used condition is that the defendant finds another individual who is prepared to vouch for his or her appearance at the end of the remand period—known as a 'surety'. The surety agrees to forfeit a sum of money to the court if the defendant absconds, ie fails to surrender to bail. The sum is set by the court and can be forfeited in whole or in part.

Quite distinct is a 'security'. The defendant deposits money or some other valuable security with the court as a guarantee that he or she will return to court—ie surrender to custody—at the end of the remand period. Ordinary bail and sureties do not involve deposits of money or valuables (in contrast to the position abroad eg American bail bonds).

Failure to surrender to bail
Failure to surrender to bail (or 'absconding') is itself a criminal offence which is punishable by magistrates by a Level 5 fine or up to three months in prison, and up to 12 months' imprisonment or an unlimited fine in the Crown Court. Magistrates have power to commit for sentence. Absconding is a ground for refusing bail in the future.

Bail information and bail support

Bail information schemes operated by the probation service exist in many magistrates' courts. These involve obtaining and verifying information about the defendant's circumstances of relevance to the bail decision and providing it to the CPS. Bail information schemes operated by the probation service, or bail units staffed by prison and probation officers, also exist in many prisons. Possibilities for bail which were not investigated before the remand to custody are pursued during a first remand to prison eg the existence of a fixed address or a surety (above). The results are placed before the court at the next remand hearing. Some areas operate 'bail support' schemes which work with bailed defendants who might otherwise be at risk of offending.

Bail hostels

The probation service manages bail hostels exclusively for people on bail and combined probation and bail hostels for those on bail, on probation or on post-custody supervision. The purpose of bail hostels is to accommodate those awaiting trial or sentence who require a high level of supervision in the community, not defendants who simply need accommodation.

Records and reasons for decisions

Broadly speaking, the Bail Act 1976 requires that where a court or constable grants or withholds bail they should make a record of the decision and, in some instances (eg where a court withholds bail), of the reasons for it; a court being obliged also to announce such reasons. In all cases, a copy of the decision must be given to the defendant on request. Where the decision is one by a magistrates' court, this enables an appeal to a Crown Court Judge (or possibly a High Court Judge if one is sitting at the local Crown Court centre).

Note: For readers requiring fuller information, a comprehensive account of the law and practice of bail is contained in *Bail: The Law, Best Practice and the Debate* by Paul Cavadino and Bryan Gibson (Waterside Press, 1993).

MODE OF TRIAL

'Mode of trial' is a key feature of the criminal justice process. It applies where the offence is triable either way: *Chapter 1*. A magistrates' court must rule on whether—on the face of the prosecutor's outline of the case—it appears to be more suitable for trial by magistrates or trial at the Crown Court. In effect, the magistrates' court must predict the likely sentence ie whether or not it is within their powers: *Chapter 9*. Whatever the magistrates' decide, the defendant has an absolute, and quite separate, right to claim trial by jury. There are two stages:

- *Mode of trial: Stage 1 'The court decides'*

The magistrates decide which mode is more suitable by taking a provisional view on the seriousness of the offence and the differing powers of magistrates and the Crown Court to impose sentence if the defendant is convicted. This is based on a summary of the case by the prosecutor and any representations which the defendant wishes to make (eg that although the offence appears to be serious it is one which raises no great complexities and is likely to be well within magistrates' maximum sentencing powers, ie up to six months in prison or 12 months if there are two or more either way offences). No reference is made to the likely plea at this stage. The Lord Chief Justice has issued *National Mode of Trial Guidelines,* which indicate matters that magistrates should take into account—both generally and in relation to particular offences.

- *Mode of trial: Stage 2 'The defendant elects'*

If the magistrates decide that the offence is more suitable for trial by them, the defendant still has an unrestricted right to elect (ie choose) between trial by magistrates and trial by jury in the Crown Court.

The defendant is first cautioned to the effect that even if trial by magistrates is chosen there is nonetheless—in the event of conviction—a power to commit to the Crown Court for sentence if six months' imprisonment turns out to be insufficient. This will usually be because of information which later emerges to justify this and which indicates that the offence is more serious than first appeared. If convicted, the defendant's previous record will be produced by the prosecutor, and this may have an effect: *Chapter 9*.

- *Mode of trial: criminal damage*

Where the alleged offence is one of criminal damage and it is unclear whether the value of the damage is over £5,000, the court can offer to treat the case as a summary matter. If the defendant rejects this it is treated as an either way offence.

TRANSFER FOR TRIAL

Where the magistrates decide at *Stage 1* above that trial by the Crown Court is more appropriate or the defendant elects trial by jury at *Stage 2*, the proceedings turn into 'transfer proceedings', ie proceedings with a view to transfer to the Crown Court for trial. 'Indictable only' offences *must* be tried in the Crown Court before a judge and jury. Preparations to transfer the case to the Crown Court for trial begin immediately and the only question for the magistrates is whether there is sufficient evidence. Transfer for trial is outlined in *Chapter 3*.

ADVANCE DISCLOSURE

Before a defendant is called upon to make any decision concerning mode of trial in respect of an either way offence, he or she is entitled to advance disclosure of the prosecution case. This is provided by the prosecutor setting out the main features of the case, usually by way of a written summary (it can, in appropriate cases, be disclosure of the entire evidence available). These particular advance disclosure procedures do not apply to purely summary offences or those which are indictable only—although prosecutors often do provide details in such cases on request. It can be noted that the defence is under no legal obligation to disclose its hand in advance of the trial (except for the defence of 'alibi' in the Crown Court and cases involving allegations of serious fraud, disclosure of official secrets or relating to the running of companies) although government proposals may alter this (see *Chapter 15*).

PRELIMINARIES

There can be several stages between the start of criminal proceedings and the time when the defendant comes to enter his or her plea to the allegation. These depend on the nature of the offence, the precise circumstances, and decisions made by the parties. Other things being equal, they will follow a fixed pattern determined locally but guided by the report of a multi-agency working party on pre-trial issues. The same report recommends maximum time periods for a range of preliminary stages.

In the Crown Court, judges hold preliminary hearings and give what are sometimes termed 'practice directions' concerning the future course of a case. Similarly, magistrates' courts may operate 'pre-trial reviews', 'preliminary hearings' or 'early administrative hearings' as appropriate. The purpose is to eliminate items which would delay the case once it reaches a court hearing.

GUILTY PLEA

The procedures in all criminal courts follow a similar pattern. Where the defendant pleads guilty, the court moves on to the sentencing stage. The facts of the case are outlined by the prosecutor and the defendant is invited to add any explanation or make representations about sentence—known as 'mitigation'. Mitigation may relate to the offence (ie the offender claims that it is less serious than might appear) or the offender (his or her personal circumstances are such that a less severe penalty should be imposed than might otherwise be appropriate). The mitigation is usually put forward on the defendant's behalf by his or her barrister or solicitor. A list of any previous convictions is handed to the court, together with other 'antecedent' information.

There may be applications for compensation to be paid to the victim of the crime (see *Chapter 18*) and for a contribution towards the costs of the prosecution. If the likely sentence is a community sentence or custody, the case will normally be adjourned for inquiries. In practice, pre-sentence reports (PSRs) will usually be needed from the probation service and possibly others. Further discussion of this aspect and of the range of sentences available is contained in *Chapter 9.*

Equivocal pleas
The court cannot accept an 'equivocal plea', ie one where the defendant pleads guilty but then adds something which indicates a defence to the allegation or that the plea is being made purely for convenience (eg 'I just want to get it over with'). Such pleas must be rejected. The case is put back, normally to a new date, for the defendant to reconsider and, if necessary, for the witnesses to be called and the case to be tried.

WRITTEN PLEAS OF GUILTY

A special 'paperwork' procedure exists in magistrates' courts which can be invoked by prosecutors in respect of minor offences. This gives the defendant an opportunity to plead 'guilty' in writing. In addition to the summons, the defendant must be served with a document called a 'statement of facts' which contains a short outline of the offence. If the defendant pleads guilty in writing, the statement of facts is then read out in court together with any mitigation and financial information put forward in writing—a form being provided for the purpose—and the court sentences in his or her absence. An application for costs can be made in writing and notice can also be served to cite any relevant previous convictions.

Where the offence is an endorsable road traffic matter, the defendant will also have to send his or her driving licence to the court for mandatory penalty points to be endorsed.

The defendant does not have to plead guilty. This is made quite clear in the accompanying notice. There are special procedures where the defendant changes his or her intentions, or turns up at court wishing to add to what has been put forward in writing. There is also flexibility, in that the court can notify the defendant that the case will be dealt with at any time within a span of 28 days.

NOT GUILTY PLEA

The procedure on a plea of 'not guilty' is broadly the same whatever the level of the offence. The presumption of innocence applies to all criminal trials. Once a 'not guilty' plea is entered, the prosecutor must establish the allegation by evidence and beyond reasonable doubt. Failing this the accused must be acquitted and discharged. The underlying principles are the same for trial by magistrates as they are for trial by jury in the Crown Court—albeit governed by separate legal provisions.

Case for the prosecution
In the normal course of events, a criminal trial opens with the prosecutor outlining the case. He or she will then call evidence to support the allegation. Usually, this will be the evidence of witnesses on the religious oath of their own choosing—or on affirmation—often called 'testimony'.

Other forms of evidence are: written statements (which can be used provided certain formalities have been complied with and the defence does not object); exhibits (eg a weapon, stolen goods, documents); and any confession to the police. Statements used in trials are known as 'section nines', after section 9 Criminal Justice Act 1982.

Criminal proceedings are adversarial in nature. At the end of each witness's evidence, the defendant or his or her advocate can cross-examine. The purpose is to challenge what was said, to cast a different light on things, to discredit the witness, to show that he or she is unreliable, or in some cases being deliberately untruthful. The prosecutor may re-examine the witness to clear up any new matters arising from cross-examination.

Witnesses are not allowed into court before they give evidence except in unusual circumstances. An example might be where a qualified expert witness is given permission to observe the evidence of other people so that he or she can comment on it in the light of his or her expertise. Qualified experts apart, evidence must be of fact, not opinion.

Refreshing memory
Testimony must be given from memory—but a witness can be given permission to refresh his or her memory from a note made at the time of the events (known as a 'contemporaneous note'). Police officers—who may attend many incidents in the course of their duties—are regularly given permission to refer to their notebooks under this rule.

Withdrawal of the case from the jury
In the Crown Court, the judge may withdraw a case from the jury where there is no basis for the prosecution to continue. There is no direct equivalent in the magistrates' court but the situation is analogous to the procedure in relation to no case to answer—save that the judge's power extends to withdrawing the case at any time if it becomes clear that there is no basis for continuing with the trial. The judge may also direct the jury to bring in a verdict of not guilty where, legally speaking, this is the correct course.

No case to answer
Before the defendant is called upon to decide whether to give evidence there must be a *prima facie* case. There will be 'no case to answer' where the prosecutor has failed to adduce any evidence of an essential element of the offence; or where the prosecution witnesses have been shown by defence cross-examination to be so unreliable that no reasonable court could convict on their evidence.

The defence may make a submission at the conclusion of the prosecution case, or the judge or magistrates can (indeed should) consider of their own motion whether there is a *prima facie* case. If not, the case ends there and then. The defendant is discharged and is normally entitled to costs from public funds. Otherwise, the case continues and the defence must decide whether or not to give evidence.

Case for the defence

The defendant in a criminal trial is not obliged to give evidence—albeit that, now the relevant provisions of the Criminal Justice and Public Order Act 1994 are in force, it is possible for inferences to be drawn if he or she remains silent either during the investigation, ie before the trial, or at it. Notwithstanding this, he or she may choose to say nothing at all. The court will then decide the case on the prosecution evidence alone. It may be eg that there is a case to answer (above) but that the evidence is weak and, even without an explanation from the defendant, incapable of satisfying the necessary standard of proof, ie beyond reasonable doubt.

If the accused elects to give evidence then the procedure is the same as that outlined in relation to prosecution evidence. The defendant gives evidence, followed by any other defence witnesses. They will all be liable to cross-examination by the prosecutor; which may be followed by re-examination.

Speeches

As already indicated, in the normal course of events the prosecutor will open the case with an outline of the allegations. The defendant or his or her representative is allowed a closing speech. This 'last word' in a criminal trial is regarded as a valuable right. But if the defendant puts forward legal argument, the prosecutor will be entitled to answer this and also to counter any false or misleading impressions, eg an incorrect summary of the evidence. Variations are possible in the order of evidence and speeches. These are beyond the scope of this introductory work.

Onus on the defendant

Just occasionally the law reverses the normal onus of proof and the defendant must establish something: see *Chapter 1.*

The court's decision

The magistrates or jury must determine guilt or innocence, basing this decision only on the evidence that it has heard. There are, in effect, three stages:

- What are the facts as accepted by the court ?
- Do the facts add up to the offence in question ?
- Is the court satisfied of guilt to the criminal standard of proof, ie beyond reasonable doubt ?

Alternative verdicts may be returned in Crown Court (and in a very limited range of situations in the magistrates' court). Thus eg, where someone is charged with murder, the jury can bring in a conviction for manslaughter. The scope for alternative verdicts rests on the nature of the original indictment or charge and the evidence in a given case. Broadly speaking, such verdicts relate to lesser offences of a similar nature disclosed by the evidence.

In the Crown Court, the judge will review the evidence and direct the jury on the law: *Chapter 3*. In the magistrates' court this dual process is the responsibility of the magistrates who 'direct themselves' albeit that in practice any legal consideration should have been drawn to their attention by the court legal advisor: *Chapter 2*.

A conviction leads to sentence. The position is then the same as when the accused pleads guilty (above) except that the court is likely to have heard far more information about the case and the defendant will have lost any advantage which might have stemmed from entering a guilty plea (ie a possible discount). Sentencing is dealt with in *Chapter 9*.

An acquittal (or 'dismissal' as it is more commonly called in magistrates' courts) results in the defendant being discharged. He or she will then normally be entitled to costs from central funds (ie public moneys).

Autrefois acquit and autrefois convict

Acquittal does not establish innocence—but it has the effect that the defendant cannot be tried again for the self-same matter. In the Crown Court, this is known as *'autrefois acquit'* and, although this plea is not technically available before magistrates, similar principles apply. Likewise, an offender cannot be convicted twice of the same matter—a previous conviction grounding a plea of *'autrefois convict'*.

CHAPTER 9

The Sentence of the Court

Sentencing is perhaps the most visible aspect of 'Law and Order'. Nowadays, it takes place against a background of public interest and concern about offending—and of criminal justice policy, as formulated by Act of Parliament and promulgated via supporting materials and ministerial pronouncements. But the courts are independent of criminal justice policy makers, the public and the media: see *Chapter 1*. Within the legal framework for sentencing, it is their task to reflect proper concern and to deal with each case on its individual merits. The special features of a case have to be balanced with the general objects of sentencing. Guideline judgments and other rulings of the Court of Appeal play a significant part in this process: see *Chapter 12*.

The main sentences currently available to the courts (July 1995) are:

- imprisonment (or detention in a young offender institution for people below 21 years of age)
- a range of community sentences including probation and community service (below)
- fines
- compensation (as a penalty in its own right or in addition to other punishment) and other orders affecting property
- a range of 'ancillary orders' such as orders for costs and disqualification eg from driving, being a company director or keeping an animal.

Maximum sentencing powers
The maximum sentence for each offence is laid down by law and the Crown Court can sentence up to this limit eg:

- life imprisonment: see under that heading below
- 14 years: house burglary, blackmail, handling stolen property
- 10 years: non-domestic burglary, obtaining by deception, criminal damage, indecent assault on a woman
- 7 years: theft, false accounting
- 5 years: causing actual bodily harm
- 2 years: carrying offensive weapon, aggravated vehicle taking.

Unlike the position in the Crown Court, the maximum term of imprisonment in the magistrates' court for an individual offence is six months regardless of any higher limits set out above; or a total of 12 months where consecutive sentences are passed for two or more either way offences as defined in *Chapter 1*. Fines and compensation each have a ceiling of £5,000 per offence. This is why the mode of trial decision is important: see *Chapter 8*.

It is common legislative practice for other powers to be fixed by reference to whether or not an offence is imprisonable (eg the power to make an attendance centre order or a community service order). Likewise, certain warrants of arrest can only be issued if an offence is imprisonable. Rights to bail are affected in a similar way.

Life sentences

Life imprisonment is the mandatory sentence for offences of murder committed by persons aged 21 and over. In the case of offenders aged 18 to 20 the equivalent mandatory sentence is called 'custody for life'; and when the offender is aged 10 to 17 the equivalent mandatory sentence is 'detention at Her Majesty's pleasure'.

Life imprisonment is also the maximum penalty which a court may pass for a number of other serious crimes, including manslaughter, robbery, rape, buggery, assault occasioning grievous bodily harm, aggravated burglary and certain firearms offences.

A life sentence is indeterminate. Some offenders spend the rest of their lives in prison, but most life sentence prisoners are eventually released on licence. In the case of mandatory life sentences, release may only be authorised by the Home Secretary following a favourable recommendation from the Parole Board. Where offenders receive discretionary life sentences for offences other than murder, the trial judge specifies a term known as the 'tariff' at the end of which the prisoner is considered for release on licence. In these cases the release decision is made by the Parole Board, which can direct the Home Secretary to release the prisoner on licence if satisfied that it is no longer necessary for the protection of the public that he or she continue to be confined. If released, a life sentence prisoner remains on licence for life and is liable to recall at any time if his or her conduct so requires.

Sentencing since 1990

The future of sentencing was explained in the white paper *Crime, Justice and Protecting the Public* (1990) which set out the government's aim that courts should deal with offenders in the community whenever possible.

A 'coherent and comprehensive' sentencing framework was introduced by the Criminal Justice Act 1991—a central intention being that a greater proportion of offenders should be dealt with by fines, compensation (which takes priority) and, where the offence was 'serious enough', community sentences involving 'restriction of liberty', some curtailment of their freedom of choice and spare time, but essentially punishment in the community. Beyond this, a custody sentence might be appropriate where the offence was 'so serious' that only such a sentence could be justified, or to protect the public from serious harm from the offender.

The 1991 Act thus represented a landmark in sentencing. It contained not just a new framework for sentencing but new concepts such as unit fines (later abolished in 1993), the idea that punishment should equate with restriction of liberty and the focusing of sentencing considerations on the current offence with a much more limited role for the offender's record.

By 1993 the government had reversed its policy at several major points. The climate of public opinion had turned against enlightened ideas in favour of instant 'solutions'. This chapter contains a description of sentencing as it now is, less than four years after the 1991 Act. Readers needing a broader analysis of the changes are referred to *Criminal Justice in Transition* (Waterside Press, 1994).

GENERAL CONSIDERATIONS

There are a number of procedures of a general nature, as distinct from those relating to a given sentence.

Previous convictions
It is the practice *after* conviction for the sentencing judge or magistrates to consider a copy of the offender's 'character and antecedents', principally containing his or her previous convictions if any. These can be taken into account when assessing the seriousness of the present offence—as can failures to respond to previous sentences. (Previous convictions are only very rarely admissible *before* conviction, eg where a defendant attacks the character of a prosecution witness, this allows his or her own character to be made known).

The Magistrates' Association has advised its members that they:

> ... should clearly identify which convictions or failures are relevant for this purpose and then consider what the effect of such convictions or failures is in relation to seriousness.

Offences taken into consideration

There is a non-statutory practice whereby a defendant may ask that outstanding offences—for which he or she has not been prosecuted—be taken into consideration when sentence is passed. This is a means of encouraging offenders to 'make a clean breast' of matters and thereby of disposing of possible further cases easily and quickly.

An application is usually only allowed where the substantive offences and the TICs are either way offences and similar in kind. Endorsable motoring offences are not allowed as TICs since the offender might thereby escape a mandatory disqualification. The defendant is usually asked to sign the list of TICs provided by the prosecutor. In the event of a refusal, the prosecutor must decide whether or not it is worth bringing separate charges or simply letting the matter drop.

Pre-sentence reports

A pre-sentence report (PSR) is essential in many cases and is the cornerstone of all the more severe forms of sentencing (but can be deemed by the court to be unnecessary in a given case). The PSR is particularly relevant where the offender is at risk of custody or where a community sentence is in prospect. PSRs are prepared by probation officer in accordance with the 'National Standard for Pre-sentence Reports'. In the youth court, the report writer may be a social worker or probation officer (who may be a member of a youth justice unit, or 'YJU'). The information in pre-sentence reports includes the following:

- An analysis of the current offence (or offences) and the circumstances leading up to it. This includes an assessment of the degree of premeditation, the impact of the offence on the victim, the offender's attitude to the offence, and any special circumstances (eg family crisis, alcohol, drugs, physical or mental health problems) which were directly relevant to the offending.

- Relevant information about the offender, including an evaluation of his or her previous patterns of offending, the results of previous sentences and any personal or social information about the offender which is relevant to past offending, to the likelihood or otherwise of reoffending or to any community sentence which the report proposes for consideration by the court.

• An assessment of the risk to the public of reoffending by the offender, including the likelihood of further offences, the nature and seriousness of such offences, the offender's capacity and motivation to change and the availability of programmes which could reduce the risk or impact of further offending.

• Information on a suitable community sentence or sentences which could be passed on the offender if the court sees fit. Where this involves probation, supervision or combination orders, the report contains an outline of the supervision plan including the aims of the programme, the methods to be used, the likely impact on offending and the steps to be taken if the offender does not comply.

Charges left on the file
In the Crown Court charges are sometimes ordered by the judge to be left on the file after the accused has been convicted of some, but not all, of the charges outstanding against him or her. Thus where, eg a substantial prison term is imposed for one or more offences and it would be pointless pursuing the remaining matters at that time these oustanding matters are left in abeyance. If that person later successfully appeals against conviction the outstanding matters might then be revived.

No separate penalty
In magistrates' courts the practice of imposing 'no separate penalty' (NSP) is regularly used and appears to have gained respectability. The device is employed when a defendant stands convicted of several offences but the totality of the offending behaviour can be dealt with by sentencing for the main offences and marking others 'NSP'. This non-statutory approach might be used, eg where there is a catalogue of motoring offences, but where justice can be done by sentencing for just some of them.

BINDING OVER TO KEEP THE PEACE

Binding over is used by magistrates' courts to mark behaviour which might lead to a breach of the peace in the future—a method known as 'preventive justice'. The power, which stems from the Justices of the Peace Act 1361, can be used on its own or, in connection with criminal offences, in addition to any penalty.

Bind overs can be made on the application (or 'complaint') of an individual—often a private individual such as a neighbour—or of the court's own motion. The main statute is still the 1361 Act, although more recent provisions regulate the procedure, and in particular applications by individuals. The individual who is bound over is required to enter into a recognisance. This is an acknowledgement of indebtedness to the Sovereign in the event of future misbehaviour. If he or she fails to keep the peace for a period fixed by the court (usually 12 months) the amount of the recognizance is at risk. A magistrates' court may order forfeiture (sometimes called 'estreatment'), in whole or in part. A refusal to be bound over is akin to contempt of court and the person concerned can be committed to custody for up to six months, or until that consent is given. However, there is a right of appeal to the Crown Court against a binding over order.

COMPENSATION

By law, compensation to a victim of crime ('the aggrieved') must come before any punishment by way of a fine. It should also be an automatic consideration in all other cases. Compensation may be used in addition to any other method of dealing with the offender, or it can stand alone as a sentence in its own right. Courts must give reasons for *not* awarding compensation in cases where they could have done so. This topic is dealt with in *Chapter 18.*

FINES

Fines are generally unlimited in the Crown Court. In the magistrates' court—where fines are regularly used for vast numbers of offences—the maximum amount of a fine is determined by reference to the one of five 'Levels', currently:

Level 1	£100
Level 2	£200
Level 3	£1,000
Level 4	£2,500
Level 5	£5,000

Guideline fines
The Magistrates' Association publishes guideline fines in its *Sentencing*

Guidelines. Most local benches also have their own guidelines—often called 'starting points', 'thinking points' or 'entry points'—descriptions which emphasise that guidelines are not to be applied in a mechanistic fashion, but subject to the exercise of judicial discretion.

Setting a fine

Fines must *reflect* the seriousness of the offence and take account of the offender's financial circumstances where these are known. Magistrates may make a financial circumstances order requiring the offender to disclose the necessary details. Failure to comply is an offence, as is making a false declaration.

Although the statutory 'unit fines' system introduced by the Criminal Justice Act 1991 was abolished in 1993, many local benches of magistrates still use informal unit fine approaches. In setting a fine, courts decide on a number of 'units' reflecting the seriousness of the offence and then calculate the size of each unit in line with the disposable income of the individual offender.

Enforcement

Financial orders, whether imposed in the Crown Court or magistrates' court, are enforced and collected by the magistrates' court. Enforcement is by way of a 'means inquiry', ie a court hearing to which the defaulter is summoned to give an explanation for non-payment. The main enforcement methods are: attachment of earnings orders (AEOs); distress warrants (ie sending in the bailiffs); money payment supervision orders (MPSOs); attachment of income support; and committal to prison.

Imprisonment in default should only be ordered where there has been wilful refusal or culpable neglect to pay—and, in effect, where the court has tried or eliminated all other methods and given the defaulter every opportunity to pay or to explain the default. The maximum term of imprisonment in default is directly related to the amount outstanding and ranges up to 45 days for fines imposed by magistrates' courts. Longer default periods can be used where the fine was imposed by the Crown Court in a substantial amount (up to 10 years). Committal can be suspended on terms, eg £5 a week, in which case the warrant will not be issued unless there is further default in payment. If there *is*, the situation must be reviewed again by the court. Failing successful representations or explanations, the warrant can then be issued. Committal in default of payment is available where the offender is aged 18 or over, but defaulters under 21 year of age are detained in young offender institutions, as opposed to a prison.

There are around 23,000 committals a year for fine default, usually for short periods. A defaulter can buy himself or herself out of prison by paying the balance due.

DISCHARGES

Discharges can be used where punishment is 'inexpedient'. There are two varieties:

Absolute discharge

An absolute discharge signifies a technical offence or extreme triviality. It puts matters at an end, and involves the offender in no further obligations or liability—other than that it ranks (as all sentences now do) as a conviction for the purposes of a criminal record.

Conditional discharge

An offender may be conditionally discharged for up to three years. The condition is that he or she does not commit another criminal offence in that period. The discharge will then lapse. If a fresh offence is committed during the period fixed by the court, the offender can be sentenced afresh for the offence in respect of which the conditional discharge was made. The offender will then face sentence for two matters, the old and the new. Conditional discharges also rank as convictions.

COMMUNITY SENTENCES

There are six community sentences. Before a community sentence can be used the offence must be 'serious enough' to justify this. The restriction of liberty imposed by the order or orders chosen must be commensurate with the seriousness of the offence and the order or orders must be the most suitable for the offender. The six community orders are:

- a probation order
- a community service order
- a combination order
- a curfew order
- an attendance centre order (under 21 years only)
- a supervision order (under 18 years only).

With the exception of curfews, each of these orders is governed by 'National Standards for the Supervision of Offenders in the Community'. Community sentences are under review. A green paper, *Strengthening Punishment in the Community*, published in March 1995, proposes replacing the present orders with a single 'community sentence' which would embrace the existing orders.

Probation

A probation order can be made for six months to three years in respect of an offender aged 16 or over. The statutory purposes are to:

- secure the rehabilitation of the offender;
- protect the public from serious harm from the offender; and
- prevent the commission by him or her of further offences.

Requirements

The order places the offender under the supervision of a probation officer. Standard conditions are attached to the order, eg to report to the probation officer as required and to receive visits at home. Extra conditions can be added and more enhanced forms of probation involve additional requirements (often called 'conditions'):

- *a requirement as to residence.* This could be:
  —residence in an approved probation hostel managed by the probation service or a voluntary organization
  —at a non-approved hostel or other institution such as a dependency clinic which may tackle drug and alcohol addictions (some of these places are private ventures)
  —a requirement to reside where directed by the probation officer. This is likely to be in the offender's home area at a private address considered suitable by the probation officer and will restrict the offender from moving without first seeking approval from the officer
- *a requirement to attend either a probation centre or other specified activities for up to 60 days*
  —a probation centre is a resource approved by the Home Secretary offering an intensive programme which addresses offending behaviour and its causes. Offenders are expected to attend for a full day (up to 60 days in all) to complete the programme
  —specified activities are approved by the local probation committee/board. Offenders can be required to attend eg an

alcohol education group, an offending behaviour group, an anger management group, a substance misuse group

—there is an exception to the 60 day maximum rule applicable to sex offenders, when there is no upper limit on the number of days for which attendance can be required (subject to not exceeding the length of the probation order)

• *a requirement to receive treatment for a mental condition.* This condition can only be used when the court has an assessment from a psychiatrist and when treatment is available. Again, the requirement can be for the whole length of the order or for a part of this time as specified by the court

• *a requirement to receive treatment for drug or alcohol dependency.* This refers to day or residential facilities—usually for the seriously addicted. There is no restriction on the length of the requirement.

The emphasis in modern probation work is on confronting offending behaviour, ie getting the offender to face up to his or her own wrongdoings.

Breach of probation
Breach of probation by failing to comply with the order renders the offender liable to a fine, community service or attendance centre (under 21 year olds only), the probation order continuing—or to the replacement of the order with a new sentence for the original offence. This will depend eg on the seriousness of the breach, the attitude of the offender and the supervising officer's assessment.

Commission of a further offence
A further offence committed during the probation period does not, in itself, render the offender liable to re-sentencing for the original offence. Everything depends on whether he or she is in breach of the requirements of the order.

Community service
Community service was introduced in 1973 as a form of punishment with in-built reparation. Community service orders (CSOs) can be made in respect of offenders aged 16 or over for between 40 and 240 hours to be completed within 12 months.

The offender carries out unpaid work in the community, several hours at a time. The offence must carry imprisonment, although the court need not have decided that imprisonment would otherwise be appropriate in this case. An assessment of the offender's suitability for the order must first be considered. Work has to be available.

Further information about the development and present day importance of community service can be found in *Paying Back: Twenty Years of Community Service* edited by Dick Whitfield and David Scott (Waterside Press, 1993).

Breach of community service
The offender can either be fined for the breach or re-sentenced for the original offence. In the first case, the order continues.

Combination order
A combination order combines between one and three years' probation with between 40 and 100 hours community service. This is the only way in which these two varieties of order can be combined. The result is likely to be a high level of restriction of liberty—and particularly if conditions are attached to the probation part of the order. Informal attempts to restrict such orders to the Crown Court would appear not to have worked and the relevant national standard now reflects the fact that such an order can properly be made in the magistrates' court.

Curfew
Courts can make curfew orders for between two and 12 hours per day for up to six months. A curfew can be coupled with electronic monitoring. Tests began in three areas in July 1995.

Attendance centre
Where the offender is under 21 an attendance centre order can be used: see under *Young Offenders,* below.

Supervision orders
Supervision orders can be made in respect of offenders below 18 years of age. These were dealt with in *Chapter 5.*

IMPRISONMENT

For imprisonment to be passed, the offence must be 'so serious' that no other sentence can be justified. The length of the sentence is also determined by the seriousness of the offence.

A special rule applies to sexual or violent offences. The court may order a prison sentence or a longer sentence than is indicated by the seriousness of the offence in order to protect the public from serious harm from the offender.

An offender can also be imprisoned if he or she refuses consent to a community sentence which requires consent.

Before a sentence of imprisonment is passed, the court must give its reasons for this. Legal aid must be offered and a PSR should normally be considered in practice (but can be dispensed with if deemed unnecessary).

Offenders below 21 years of age cannot be sent to prison but are sentenced to detention in a young offender institution (below).

Suspended sentences of imprisonment

Imprisonment may be suspended for between one and two years. The court must first be sure that imprisonment is appropriate—and then go on to decide that, in the circumstances, it is correct to suspend its operation. The court must be of the opinion that there are 'exceptional circumstances' for the suspension. If it suspends the sentence, the court must go on to consider imposing a fine and compensation. Reasons must still be announced where imprisonment is suspended.

If the offender commits another imprisonable offence within the operational period of the suspended sentence, the sentence falls to be activated. Normally it will be activated unless there is a good reason for not doing so. That reason must be given in court. The court can in appropriate circumstances: take no action; alter the operational period (including, in effect, re-starting it for a new two year period); or activate the sentence for a shorter term than that originally imposed and suspended. An activated sentence can be concurrent or consecutive to any new sentence of imprisonment.

The Crown Court can make a suspended sentence supervision order, ie an order that the probation service supervise the offender during the period of the suspended sentence.

COMMITTAL FOR SENTENCE

Where the offender is aged 18 or over, the offence is triable either way and it has been dealt with summarily by the magistrates' court, the court can still commit to the Crown Court for sentence if it decides that its own powers of punishment are insufficient—in effect where the offence turns out to be more serious than first appeared or where the public needs to be protected from a sexual or violent offender for longer than six months (12 months in aggregate).

COSTS AND WITNESS EXPENSES

Costs including witness expenses may be awarded against either party according to the outcome of the case and events which have occurred during the proceedings.

Where a defendant is acquitted, or the case is withdrawn, abandoned or discontinued for any reason, he or she is normally entitled to costs from central funds (ie public moneys). Costs can be ordered to be paid by the Crown Prosecution Service, police or other prosecutor in appropriate cases. Conversely, a convicted defendant might normally expect to have to pay all or part the costs of the prosecution including those of any civilian witnesses who attended court to give evidence.

OTHER ANCILLARY ORDERS

Apart from costs, other ancillary orders include such matters as: driving disqualification or the endorsement of penalty points on a driving licence; other disqualifications eg from being a company director following a conviction for fraud; and restitution orders in respect of stolen property or forfeiture orders in respect of a range of articles such as offensive weapons, drugs, and implements used to commit or attempt crime: see *Chapter 18.*

MENTAL DISORDER

Mental disorder can impinge on a criminal trial at several points. An accused person may be unfit to plead, or may raise a defence of insanity—either of which will normally result in that person being detained without limit of time. Diminished responsibility, which may be transient, is a defence to murder and, if successful reduces a conviction to manslaughter thereby giving the judge a discretion concerning the length of sentence (as opposed to a mandatory life sentence for murder: see above).

The Mental Health Act 1983 allows courts to deal with cases in a variety of ways when problems arise from the defendant's mental state. These include: hospital orders and guardianship orders—but conditions of treatment can also be attached to probation orders (above). Reports are obtained from psychiatrists before any decision is made and a court which is considering sending someone to prison who appears to be suffering from mental disorder must first obtain and consider such a report. Where an offender is sent to a hospital, a judge of the Crown Court can make an order restricting that person's discharge by the authorities. These important but specialist areas are beyond the scope of this introductory work.

YOUNG OFFENDERS

Offenders aged 18 but under 21 are generally called 'young offenders' or 'young adult offenders' as opposed to 'adults' (21 and over) or 'children' and 'young persons' (below 18: see *Chapter 5*). The underlying position in relation to the 18 to 20 age group is broadly the same as that in relation to offenders aged 21 and over set out above. Thus eg they can be placed on probation and given community service orders. However:

- *Detention in a young offender institution*
In place of prison offenders under 21 can be ordered to be detained in a young offender institution. The minimum sentence is 21 days (two months for under 18 year olds). As with imprisonment, magistrates' maximum powers are six months, or 12 months where there are two or more either way offences. There is power to commit to the Crown Court for sentence. The restrictions on custody are the same as for imprisonment. Again, courts must give reasons for using custody and explain these in 'ordinary language'. The court must obtain a PSR unless it considers this to be unnecessary (which, given the age of offenders in this category, would be unusual); and must offer legal aid.

- *No suspended sentences*
It not possible to pass a suspended sentence of detention in a young offender institution.

- *Attendance centre*
Depending on local availability, these are centres where offenders attend for two or three hours at a time for a mix of rigorous physical activity and instruction. Attendance centres are administered by the Home Office and are usually run by the police, often on a Saturday afternoon. They may be single sex,

or mixed centres. Those for this age group are known as 'senior attendance centres'.

The offence must be imprisonable—but attendance centre orders can also be used for non-payment of fines and breach of probation whether the original offence was imprisonable or not.

The maximum aggregate hours of attendance is 36 and the minimum 12. There are limits on the distance that the offender may travel and on the time that this takes—usually 15 miles and/or one and a quarter hours. Offenders pay their own travelling costs and journey times come on top of the hours in the order.

EARLY RELEASE FROM PRISON

Since 1992, courts have had extensive powers to deal with breach of licence by offenders released from prison under the early release scheme. Breach of licence is normally dealt with by the magistrates' court but there is power to commit to the Crown Court in certain circumstances. The probation service supervises offenders released on licence after serving the custodial part of their sentence. The procedures involve assessment of the risk to the public and speedy action if licence conditions are not complied with.

A note on parole
Parole (which, to all intents, has now been replaced by conditional release) was introduced in 1968. Parole could be granted to a prisoner, following a selection procedure, after the prisoner had served one third of his or her sentence, or 12 months, whichever was the longer. Twelve months was the 'minimum qualifying period' but in 1984 the 'minimum qualifying period' was reduced to six months, making many more prisoners eligible. Prisoners released on parole were subject to 'parole licence' with fairly strict conditions and a speedy recall procedure.

In theory the Home Secretary was responsible for every decision, following Parole Board recommendations; but in practice many cases of short sentence prisoners were decided by local review committees (now obsolete).

The Carlisle report
In 1987 Lord Carlisle of Bucklow QC began work as chairman of a review committee to consider the parole system—the first in-depth review since its inception. The committee's terms of reference required

it to include an examination of the relationship between sentences passed and time actually spent in custody.

The Carlisle report was presented to Parliament in November 1988 and laid the foundations for the current system of 'early release on licence' which was incorporated into the Criminal Justice Act 1991. The new system is outlined below. (In theory now, except for those people sentenced before 1 October 1992, there is no such thing as parole. In practice, the expression 'parole' remains in common usage). The Parole Board still functions, but it is the discretionary conditional release scheme that it now oversees.

Early release
A basic premise of the Carlisle Report was that a prison sentence should be served partly *in custody* and partly *in the community*—with the offender under some form of sanction for the whole of the sentence as awarded in court. No prisoners are now released until they have served at least 50 per cent of their sentences (plus any 'additional days' imposed as a punishment for offences against prison discipline). Many prisoners are thus released on licence to probation service supervision without going through any selection procedure at all. Others go through such a procedure and are considered either suitable or unsuitable (see *DCR* below). In outline, the position is as follows:

ACR (12 months but under four years)
• Firstly, automatic conditional release (or ACR) cases. The prisoners concerned are released automatically under supervision but without a selection procedure at the half-way point of their sentences (subject to 'additional days' which can be awarded as punishment for prison disciplinary offences).

DCR (four years and over)
• Secondly, discretionary conditional release (or DCR) cases. These prisoners are selected by the parole board to be released on licence at or after the half-way point of the sentence until the three quarter stage of their sentence. Those *not* selected are automatically discharged at the two thirds stage to be on licence until the three-quarter point. This category could include some very serious offenders.

Aims of post-release supervision
The ''National Standard for Supervision Before and After Release from Custody' states that the overall aims are:

91

- protection of the public
- prevention of re-offending
- successful re-integration of the offender into the community.

As well as setting out frequency of contact and targets, the supervision plan should identify resources which will:

- confront offending behaviour—challenging the offender to accept responsibility for his or her crime and its consequences
- make offenders aware of the impact of the crimes they have committed on their victims, themselves and the community
- motivate and assist the offender towards a greater sense of personal responsibility, to aid re-integration as a law abiding member of the community
- remedy practical obstacles which impede rehabilitation—eg education, training, skills needed for employment, and action to counter drug or alcohol misuse, illiteracy or homelessness.

Failure to comply with post-custody supervision
Failure to comply with the conditions of post-custody supervision will lead to breach action. The procedures are as follows:

Automatic conditional release
For offenders on ACR, action is taken through the magistrates' court. The court has the power to allow the licence to continue without penalty; or to fine and allow the licence to continue; or to return the offender to prison for up to six months. It may commit to the Crown Court where a longer return to prison is considered appropriate.

Discretionary conditional release
For offenders on DCR, the matter is reported to the Parole Board via the Home Office parole unit. The Board can order recall to prison or issue warning letters. The Board may also be informed and asked to take action where:

- situations arise concerning the offender's behaviour such that further serious offences are likely to be committed
- it appears that the safety of the public may be at risk
- the offender's behaviour, although not involving a direct risk to the safety of the public, seems likely to bring the licence

system into disrepute, or to create general difficulty in the supervision of offenders if action is not seen to be taken.

There are special provisions for the addition and deletion of special conditions in both ACR and DCR licences and emergency recall facilities in relation to DCR cases.

Young offenders

The conditional release system applies to young people serving sentences of detention in a young offender institution of 12 months or more. Those serving less than 12 months will be subject to a period of supervision on release of not less than three months. As in ACR cases, breach is dealt with through the magistrates' court. Supervision is carried out by social services or the probation service.

'Life licence'

Prisoners sentenced to life imprisonment ('lifers') are subject to continuous review and, depending on progress, a downgrading of their prison category. Because of the length of the sentence—the average length of time served is over 14 years and in some cases life means for life—it is likely that several probation officers will be involved in the sentence plan and the throughcare process.

Release cannot take place until the end of the 'tariff' period. In a mandatory life-sentence for murder, the tariff is decided upon by the Home Secretary with advice from the trial judge and the Lord Chief Justice. At the end of the tariff period, the Home Secretary cannot release the prisoner unless the Parole Board recommends this. In the case of discretionary life sentences, ie imposed for offences other than murder, the trial judge fixes the tariff period, at the end of which the decision to release is made by a 'Discretionary Lifer Panel' of the Parole Board, consisting of a High Court Judge, a psychiatrist or probation officer, and a lay person or a probation officer.

Life-sentence prisoners are released on licence. Although the requirement to report to a supervising probation officer can be removed after a period, the licence remains in force during the offender's lifetime. At any time, the licence can be revoked and the lifer returned to prison.

Conditionally discharged patients from mental hospitals

An offender who is adjudged to be seriously mentally ill and who poses a serious risk to the public can be made the subject of a restriction order for a specified period or indefinitely by the Crown Court under section

41 Mental Health Act 1983. In due course, the Home Secretary has the power to order that:

- the restriction order should cease to have effect; and
- the patient should be discharged absolutely; or
- the patient should be subject to conditions and the possibility of being recalled.

It is likely that supervision will be by a local psychiatrist *and* a 'social supervisor' who can be a probation officer or a local authority social worker. The discharged patient must live at an agreed address and is likely to be on supervision for at least two years. Concern about the patient can lead to the psychiatrist using his or her civil power to admit the patient to hospital compulsorily, and ultimately the Home Office can order a recall.

Voluntary after-care

The possibility of *voluntary* aftercare arises where the sentence is too short for ACR, ie less than 12 months. There is then a statutory duty on probation officers to provide assistance if the released prisoner requests it. Such prisoners are released at the half-way stage of their sentence (subject to any 'additional days' imposed as a punishment for prison disciplinary offences). They make contact with the probation service on a purely voluntary basis—something which is not uncommon in practice.

Note: A comprehensive analysis of the sentencing provisions outlined in this chapter—and the changes which took place between 1991 and 1994—is contained in *Criminal Justice in Transition* (Waterside Press, 1994). An outline of sentencing in magistrates' courts can be found in *The Sentence of the Court: A Handbook for Magistrates* written by Michael Watkins, Winston Gordon and Anthony Jeffries—and produced under the auspices of the Justices' Clerks' Society (Waterside Press, 1995).

CHAPTER 10

Appeals

Various channels of appeal are open to people who convicted and sentenced by magistrates or by the Crown Court. Appeals may be against conviction or sentence and may be based on fact or law.

APPEALS TO THE COURT OF APPEAL

Anyone who is convicted and sentenced by the Crown Court can appeal to the Criminal Division of the Court of Appeal against conviction, sentence or both. The Court of Appeal (Criminal Division) is situated in the Royal Courts of Justice in London. Courts are constituted by the Lord Chief Justice and Lords Justices of Appeal assisted by High Court judges as required.

A further appeal may be made to the House of Lords when it has been certified by the Court of Appeal that a point of law of general public importance was involved in the decision and either the Court of Appeal or the House of Lords grants leave to appeal.

Appeals against conviction

A defendant may appeal against his or her conviction as of right on any question of law alone (eg whether the judge properly defined the ingredients of the offence to the jury). In cases which involve questions of fact (eg whether the jury should have convicted on the evidence) the offender may only appeal if he or she obtains a certificate from the trial judge that the case is fit for appeal or, more usually, obtains leave from the Court of Appeal.

The Court of Appeal may allow the appeal on one of the following grounds :

- that the conviction should be set aside on the grounds that under all the circumstances of the case it is unsafe or unsatisfactory
- that the judgment of the court of trial should be set aside on the grounds of a wrong decision of any question of law
- that there was a material irregularity in the course of the trial.

The court may dismiss an appeal when, although there has been a wrong decision on a point of law or an irregularity in the trial, it considers that no miscarriage of justice has actually occurred. These grounds will be altered when the Criminal Appeal Act 1995 becomes law: this will replace the above provisions with a requirement that the Court of Appeal shall allow an appeal against conviction if it thinks that the conviction is unsafe.

Appeal against sentence
Appeals against sentence to the Court of Appeal always require the leave of the Court of Appeal. The Court may quash a sentence imposed by the Crown Court and in its place substitute any sentence which that court could have imposed. It must so exercise its powers that, taking the case as a whole, the applicant is not more severely dealt with on appeal than he or she was dealt with by the Crown Court.

Application for leave to appeal
In order to obtain leave from the Court of Appeal, the appellant must within 28 days of conviction or sentence file an application for leave and notice of the grounds of appeal. The application is considered by one judge who is known as the 'single judge'. This consideration takes place on the basis of a written application for leave and any supporting material sent in with it.

If the single judge refuses the application, the appellant may apply to the full court against that decision. In order to discourage appellants who have no chance of success, the single judge or the full court may direct that time spent in custody pending the appeal hearing shall not count towards the sentence. However, this power is not often exercised.

Procedure on appeal
The hearing of the appeal is by a court of three judges. They will have received a note on the case prepared by a barrister employed by the Court of Appeal, which will set out a summary of the facts and arguments. Counsel on behalf of the appellant and the respondent address the Court and the decision is by a majority.

Rulings of the Court of Appeal and Practice Directions
Rulings are regularly reported in law reports (see *Chapter 1*). These form a corpus of information about sentencing, against which background all courts then operate. Judgments by the Court of Appeal can have substantial impact on sentencing, particularly guideline judgments

which set out detailed guidance on a particular area of sentencing: eg the judgement in the *Billam* case in 1986 substantially increased lengths of sentence for rape offences.

Closely allied to appeal rulings but not stemming from an individual case are Practice Directions setting out advice on a given aspect of law and procedure.

Appeals from the Crown Court by way of case stated

Where the Crown Court is sitting to hear appeals from magistrates' courts (below), its decisions cannot be challenged in the Court of Appeal. However, the appellant has the right to apply for a case to be stated by the Crown Court for the determination of a point of law by the High Court. Such appeals are heard by a Divisional Court of the Queen's Bench Division: see below.

Intervention by the Home Secretary

The Home Secretary may consider representations and intervene in cases tried on indictment when appeal rights have been exhausted. This is normally done only if there is new evidence or some other consideration of substance which was not before the original trial court. In such cases the Home Secretary refers the matter to the Court of Appeal. This power of the Home Secretary will shortly be superseded by a new Criminal Cases Review Commission: see *Chapter 15.*

The Attorney General's powers

The Attorney General may seek a ruling of the Court of Appeal on a point of law which has been material in a case where a person is tried on indictment. The Court of Appeal has power to refer the point to the House of Lords if necessary. The ruling will constitute a binding precedent, but an acquittal in the original case is not affected.

The Attorney General also has power to refer a case to the Court of Appeal if he considers that a sentence passed by the Crown Court for an offence triable only on indictment, or for certain offences which are triable either way (eg threats to kill, cruelty to or neglect of children, and serious fraud), was unduly lenient. The Court of Appeal may increase sentence within the statutory maximum for the offence.

APPEALS AGAINST MAGISTRATES' DECISIONS

Anyone who has been convicted and sentenced by a magistrates' court can appeal to the Crown Court against the conviction, sentence, or both or to the High Court on a point of law. The prosecutor cannot appeal against an acquittal, or against what he or she believes to be an over-lenient sentence (this form of appeal is currently restricted to certain sentences imposed by the Crown Court: above).

Appeal to the Crown Court

This is the normal method of appeal against a decision by magistrates. The convicted person must give notice of appeal within 21 days of being sentenced. This period can be extended by the Crown Court (called 'leave to appeal out of time'). The notice of appeal must set out the details of the conviction and sentence and state the grounds of appeal.

- *Appeal against conviction*

Appeals against conviction are heard by a Judge sitting with two magistrates (usually: there can be up to four magistrates). There is no jury. The case is heard afresh. The Crown Court either upholds the conviction or substitutes an acquittal. If the Crown Court convicts the accused it then proceeds to sentence.

- *Appeal against sentence*

Similarly, an appeal against sentence is heard by a Judge and two magistrates. The court is addressed by the appellant (ie the person making the appeal) or his or her legal representative. The Crown Court can confirm the decision or substitute its own sentence, either a more severe or lesser one—but limited to magistrates' maximum powers of punishment as described in *Chapter 5.*

Appeal to the Divisional Court

Appeals on points of law go to the Queen's Bench Division of the High Court of Justice (QBD)—where they are heard by a 'Divisional Court' of the QBD. The court is presided over by the Lord Chief Justice of the day, who on some occasions sits in person to hear cases from magistrates' courts. Appeals may involve points of law of general importance the outcome of which will have widescale effects: eg a decision that an individual magistrates' court has not followed correct procedures could invalidate many cases which have been dealt with nation-wide.

Usually, three High Court Judges sit to hear such appeals—which are open to both the defendant and the prosecutor. Rulings (or 'judgments') of the Divisional Court constitute legally binding precedents which must be followed by all courts in future. They are reported in the law reports and noted in practitioner textbooks: see the common examples of such works quoted in *Chapter 10*.

There are three methods of challenging a decision by magistrates in the High Court:

• *Case stated*

Here, the magistrates state a case for the opinion of the High Court. This involves setting down in writing what facts the magistrates found to exist in the case and then saying what law or legal principles they applied to those facts. The Divisional Court either upholds the magistrates' decision or makes some other order, eg quashing the conviction; or ordering the magistrates to rehear the case applying the law correctly. There is a timetable for the various stages. The process starts with an application by *either* party for the magistrates to state a case for the opinion of the High Court—which must be made within 21 days of the final decision by the magistrates court. Magistrates can refuse a 'frivolous' application, or ask the applicant to identify the point of law involved eg where they are unable to discern a legal issue which actually bore on the decision.

• *Judicial review*

Anyone who is aggrieved by a decision of magistrates (which can extend beyond the parties themselves to other people with a legitimate interest in the outcome of the case—what is called *locus standi*) may ask the Divisional Court to review the case in order to see whether eg the court acted judicially, fairly, without bias, observing principles of natural justice, or whether it followed the correct procedures. If it did not, the remedy is one or more of the 'prerogative orders': *certiorari* to quash a decision; *mandamus* to compel the magistrates' court to act (eg by hearing the case in a proper manner); and *prohibition* to prevent magistrates acting in error. Judicial review must normally be pursued within six months.

• *Declarations*

More rare, are applications to the Divisional Court by either party for that court merely to declare what the law is on a particular point, or what it means. The magistrates' court then acts on the advice given.

Appeals to the High Court are generally understood to be appeals against the legal advice which was given by the legal advisor to the court—although magistrates have been known to reject that advice and in some of these instances to put themselves at risk of having to pay the costs of the proceedings personally—assuming that the advisor was right and they were wrong. There is a high risk that this would happen if the point at issue is already well settled.

Rectification of mistakes
Both the Crown Court and the magistrates' court possess certain powers to correct their own mistakes—short of matters which need to go to a higher court on appeal.

Free pardon
Free pardons are awarded by the Sovereign. This might occur, eg where the normal appeal mechanisms are exhausted, or they cannot be used for some reason eg because the time limit for an appeal has expired but facts affecting conviction have only just surfaced. Similarly, it might transpire that the defendant should never have been punished eg delegated legislation may have been invalid from the outset. Strictly, a pardon does not remove a conviction; but it erases the consequences.

Part III

Key Actors

CHAPTER 11

Before Court

There is a nation-wide network of law enforcement agencies, investigators or prosecutors in England and Wales. Investigation is carried out principally by the ordinary police forces (sometimes called the civil police) but also by a collection of specialist police forces and a number of organizations which are charged with the oversight of specific kinds of offence such as the evasion of excise duty or health and safety at work offences. The Crown Prosecution Service (dealt with in *Chapter 12*) has both advisory and prosecution decision-making functions.

THE POLICE

There are 43 police forces in England and Wales. They each cover a county or group of counties, except in London where one force covers the City and the Metropolitan Police covers the rest.

The main aims of the police service, as set out in the White Paper *Police Reform* (1993), are to:

- fight and prevent crime;
- uphold the law;
- bring to justice those who break the law;
- protect, help and reassure the community; and
- provide good value for money.

Every police force is divided geographically into a number of areas or divisions, each based on a divisional police station. These stations have facilities for charging people, cells, a Criminal Investigations Department (CID) office and a communications room. The areas in turn are usually divided into sub-divisions, based on sub-divisional police stations.

In addition to employing police officers, police forces also employ civilians in administrative and other posts, thereby releasing officers for operational duties. The police also recruit and use 'special constables' (part-time volunteers) acting in support of regular officers.

Political accountability

The police are politically accountable through a tripartite structure consisting of the chief constable, the police authority and the Home Secretary.

In all forces, the chief constable (commissioner in London) is responsible for all aspects of the conduct of his or her force. The chief constable has the power to appoint, promote and discipline officers below the rank of assistant chief constable. He or she also has a duty to enforce the law: broadly, to bring to justice those who have broken it.

Chief constables and police authorities

Chief constables are appointed by and make reports to their local police authorities. Until recently these were made up of local councillors and magistrates. The police authorities fix the maximum strength of the force, subject to approval by the Government, and provide buildings and equipment. They can advise a chief constable on matters such as law enforcement, policing priorities and the allocation and deployment of police resources. The Police and Magistrates' Courts Act 1994 made police authorities free-standing bodies, reduced their size and introduced independent members in addition to local councillors and magistrates.

The Home Secretary and the Home Office

The Home Secretary is the police authority for the Metropolitan Police. (He has appointed a Metropolitan Police Committee to advise him in this role). He can make regulations covering: qualifications for appointment, promotion and retirement; discipline; hours of duty, leave, pay and allowances; uniform; and ranks. He also has various powers to influence practice nationally, for example by participating in senior appointments and by issuing circulars, which forces are expected to comply with, on the general direction of policing policy.

The Police Department of the Home Office supports the Home Secretary in the discharge of his responsibilities to promote police efficiency and effectiveness. It provides the administrative framework which enables government policy on policing to be formulated and implemented, and it provides central services to the police.

The Home Secretary also influences policy through HM Inspectorate of Constabulary. The Inspectorate carries out full primary inspections, which cover all aspects of force organization and activity; performance review inspections which concentrate in greater depth on a limited number of issues; and thematic inspections which examine a specific issue across a number of forces (eg the police use of firearms). Her Majesty's Chief Inspector of Constabulary is also the Home Secretary's senior professional adviser on police matters including senior appointments.

Police officers are not allowed to join a trade union or go on strike. All ranks, however, have their own staff associations.

POLICE WORK

The police have a duty to maintain law and order, to protect people and property, to prevent crime and, when it occurs, to try to detect offenders and prepare case papers with a view to prosecution. They control road traffic and advise local authorities on traffic questions. They also carry out certain duties, such as immigration enquiries, for the government. By long tradition they assist anyone who needs their help and they deal with emergencies.

Much of this work (aspects of which are described below) is carried out by patrol officers, who make up around 60 per cent of force strength. They are deployed on foot or in vehicle patrols and are organized on the basis of beats. Ordinary beat officers normally work a shift or relief. Officers are not usually assigned to a particular beat: they go wherever they are needed. More specialised work is undertaken by operational officers, who make up a third of force strength.

Maintaining public order
The maintenance of public order ranges from the day-to-day policing of the streets to the control of football crowds and demonstrators.

Patrol officers are supported by special patrol groups or task forces, officers seconded from the divisions who are specially trained and equipped and put on standby to respond to any incident or potential disorder. Forces also have Police Support Units (PSUs), which are made up of ordinary officers who carry out normal policing duties but who are given special training in the use of shields and riot techniques. PSUs will aid other forces in emergencies. The Metropolitan Police also has District Support Units, mobile instant response units who patrol the streets in vans.

Since the 1981 urban riots, the police have been given more powers and equipment to deal with disorders, and more resources have been devoted to public order training.

Preventing crime

The main responsibility within police forces for crime prevention lies with patrol officers. While they may rarely discover 'invisible' (ie off-street) crimes such as burglary, it is argued that their presence on the streets may reduce the number of 'visible' crimes and reduce the fear of crime. In addition to these officers, every force employs crime prevention officers in their own right. These officers carry out security surveys of domestic and commercial premises and advise on appropriate security, and distribute crime prevention publicity.

Forces are also involved in a range of other crime prevention initiatives. They help to establish neighbourhood watch schemes, which involve neighbours keeping watch for people acting suspiciously and promote household security measures such as property marking. Other watches have been formed based on similar principles. These include boat, business, cab, campus, caravan, child, farm, hospital, pub, school and shop watches.

Many forces work with other agencies in analysing and tackling local crime problems—eg on run-down housing estates and school premises. Some have launched initiatives to protect elderly people, or to involve young people in activities and education programmes.

Some police officers give up part of their spare time to supervise young offenders given attendance centre orders by the courts. These orders aim to deprive young offenders of some of their leisure time and encourage them to make more constructive use of it.

INVESTIGATING CRIME

Minor crime is investigated by uniformed patrol officers including, in some forces, officers designated as beat crimes officers. Broadly, plain-clothes CID officers take over the investigation of more complex and serious crimes after an initial assessment by uniformed officers.

CID officers are usually based at sub-divisional or divisional police stations or in central specialist sections, such as a stolen vehicles squad, a commercial fraud squad, a 'special branch' (responsible for dealing with threats to public order, espionage, sabotage, 'subversive activities', immigration, personnel, protection etc), a robbery squad, a drugs squad (see below), a serious crimes squad and a cheque fraud squad. These squads are supported by a number of services such as the criminal intelligence section (which collects and circulates information relating to crime), scenes of crimes officers, fingerprint and photographic officers, firearms and explosives section, prosecutions section, and a criminal records office. CID officers may also be seconded to their regional crime squads, which deal with crimes covering more than one force area.

With Customs and Excise, the police have established a National Drugs Intelligence Unit which gathers, collates and circulates information on drug misuse. A financial section receives information from banks and other financial institutions about funds suspected of having been derived from drug trafficking. This information is checked out and passed to operational officers.

The central drugs squad in London and the drugs wings of the regional crime squads investigate national and international drug trafficking. In addition, every force has a local drugs squad which tackles middle-level dealers in their areas, often in co-operation with the regional drug wings. At a divisional level, local uniformed and plain-clothes officers deal with individual misusers and street pushers in the normal course of their duties.

Crimes are most likely to be solved where the victim or police know the identity of the offender from the outset or when the offender is caught at the scene of the crime.

Helping victims

Police can play an important role in reassuring and advising victims of crime on matters such as personal safety, security precautions, court procedures, getting compensation through the Criminal Injuries Compensation Scheme, and details of local victim support schemes.

The police have become more aware of the particular needs of victims of serious sexual assault and child abuse, of domestic violence, and of racial harassment and attacks. Increasingly, female victims of sexual assaults have been dealt with by female officers and female police doctors. All forces have set up units within their CID to deal with cases of child abuse and are working with other agencies to help the victims. Better interviewing and examination techniques have been introduced, along with a policy to protect and care for victims in a way which minimises further distress.

Forces have been given guidance on recognising victims of domestic violence. Some forces have set up domestic violence units. More forces are training officers to respond swiftly and sympathetically to racial incidents and to feed back details of the investigation to the victim. The Association of Chief Police Officers (ACPO) has produced a definition of 'racial incidents' wide enough to include any incident where the victim or anyone else perceives racial motivation.

Public relations

Overall, public confidence in the police is high. However, surveys have found that attitudes to the police differ strikingly according to age, race, gender and area of residence. Research shows that a substantial proportion of the black population lacks confidence and trust in the police. This applies not only to the young but also to middle-aged and older black people and is the case for both Afro-Caribbean and Asian people, although there are differences in the way the problem is experienced.

The police have two distinct roles in their relationship with the public. They police the public—they stop, question, control, arrest, summon, detain and apply a variety of sanctions against certain members of the public. The police also provide services to the public— in particular, they maintain public order and detect offenders on behalf of the public (above).

The police must been seen to carry out their policing role fairly. Towards this end, the Police and Criminal Evidence Act 1984 (PACE) has regulated police powers on the streets, on premises and at the police station. Lay visitor schemes have been introduced to assess and report on conditions of detention in police stations and on the way in which the rules governing the treatment of detained people are applied.

Most forces now have specialist community liaison officers whose remit is to develop contacts with voluntary and statutory agencies, ethnic minority organisations and schools. Under PACE, police authorities are required to consult local people about the policing of their area. As a result all police authorities have set up consultative committees on which are represented police authority members, police officers, councillors, statutory and voluntary agencies and community groups.

The police's ability to carry out their policing role depends to a large extent on public co-operation, and this is more likely to be forthcoming if the police are seen to be responding sufficiently vigorously to their priorities. The public want more officers on foot patrol and the police to be more responsive to calls for help. The police have responded by deploying more officers on foot patrols and changing shift systems to ensure that police cover more accurately reflects public needs. In addition to ordinary patrol officers, forces also deploy home beat officers. These officers are given responsibility for a particular beat and are expected to get to know the people who live and work on it. They may be expected to maintain regular contact with local schools, collect information about racial incidents and have responsibility for investigating minor burglaries on their beat.

Complaints

A complaint about the police may be informally resolved between the police and complainant or formally investigated by the police. It can be considered for informal resolution if it would not justify criminal disciplinary proceedings. If the complainant agrees to informal resolution, a senior officer will investigate and mediate between the complainant and the officer(s) subject to the complaint. If mediation fails, another officer will be appointed to deal with the complaint formally.

The Police Complaints Authority must supervise the police investigation of very serious complaints. It may supervise other complaints if it considers it desirable and in the public interest to do so. Some people sue the police for damages as an alternative to the police complaints procedure.

SPECIAL POLICE FORCES

There are a number of special police forces such as the Ministry of Defence police and British Transport police, each of which has powers analogous to the civil police but within a given sphere of activity.

THE POLICE AND PROSECUTION

A principal function of the police where a crime is detected is to decide whether or not to arrest the suspect, to make inquiries (*Chapter 6*) and to decide whether to launch a prosecution. In terms of the future course of a criminal case, the police will also gather the evidence which is necessary to support a prosecution, often in the form of witness statements and exhibits: see *Chapter 8*. This will also involve incidental decisions about whether the suspect or accused person should be granted bail (the police now have powers to grant both ordinary bail and conditional bail) or whether he or she should be brought before a court with a view to an application being made for a remand in custody, or where the police are unsure about whether bail should be granted, or where they wish to see conditions imposed in relation to matters which are beyond their powers eg residence in a hostel: see *Chapter 8*.

Prosecution or diversion
Even where there is clear evidence to support the initiation of a prosecution, the police may decide against that course in favour of a formal caution or other form of diversion from the criminal justice process: see *Chapter 7*.

Fixed penalties
Police, traffic wardens and others are given statutory power to adopt schemes in relation to minor offences whereby offenders are issued with a fixed penalty, either at the time of an offence or thereafter. This again avoids the need for prosecution provided that the penalty is paid within the period specified in the notice, usually 28 days.

Mitigated penalties
Some prosecutors, such as the Inland Revenue and Customs and Excise, may accept a 'mitigated penalty' in lieu of formal action, not unlike a fixed penalty but usually in a substantial amount.

OTHER AGENTS OF LAW ENFORCEMENT

Among the many other agents of law enforcement which have an investigative and prosecution function are the following:

- the Serious Fraud Office (SFO). The SFO is headed by a Director of Serious Fraud and has authority to take over prosecutions from other agencies where the matter falls within its remit.
- Customs and Excise responsible for ports, airports, drug trafficking, rivers and tunnels; such items as the seizure of drug-related cash; and non-payment or evasion of Value Added Tax (VAT)
- the Health and Safety Executive which deals not only with everyday prosecutions of employers for run-of-the-mill failures to comply with safety legislation but also with cases eg where a fatality has occurred or where the defect complained of may require the changing of manufacturing practices nation-wide
- TV Licence Records Office which prosecutes people for having no TV licence
- local authorities who (apart from bringing civil care proceedings in respect of children and having responsibility

108

for vulnerable adults) have a number of prosecution functions, eg the enforcement of bye-laws; consumer protection (ie 'trading standards' and the protection of people from misrepresentations and misdescriptions of products offered for sale); and school attendance

- the National Society for the Prevention of Cruelty to Children (NSPCC)
- the Royal Society for the Protection of Animals (RSPCA).

CHAPTER 12

In Court

JUDGES

Every criminal court above the magistrates' court relies on professional judges drawn from the legal profession, principally from leading practitioners at the Bar—although, increasingly judges have been appointed from the ranks of solicitors. All judges are appointed by the sovereign on the recommendation of the Lord Chancellor as head of the judiciary. In the case of the most senior appointments, those to the Court of Appeal and House of Lords, the recommendation is routed via the Prime Minister.

Law Lords
The judges of the House of Lords are known as Lords of Appeal in Ordinary. On appointment they become life peers. By convention, they do not participate in the general business of the House except where there is a legal or judicial interest. The Law Lords who number between nine and eleven sit as an Appellate Committee of the House in an ante-room (as opposed to the chamber of the House) to hear appeals from, as well as other non-criminal courts, the Court of Appeal (Criminal Division) and the Queen's Bench Division of the High Court of Justice. The Lord Chancellor is the head of this Committee and may sit from time to time.

Lords Justices of Appeal
Each of the 29 judges of the Court of Appeal is known as 'Lord Justice'. Lords Justices are promoted from among High Court Judges. They sit regularly in the Civil Division of the Court of Appeal and some also sit in the Criminal Division.

High Court judges
There are 95 High Court judges who, as well as sitting in the High Court, may also sit in the Crown Court. At those Crown Court centres where a High Court judge sits, cases are assigned between different types of judges on the principle that the High Court judge should try the more serious or difficult cases.

The Lord Chancellor appoints High Court judges who are selected almost entirely from among senior barristers (normally Queen's Counsel, ie 'QCs') although solicitors are now also eligible for appointment.

Circuit judges, recorders and assistant recorders

The Lord Chancellor appoints circuit judges, recorders and assistant recorders to sit in the Crown Court.

Circuit judges, who sit in one of the six 'circuits' in England and Wales, are drawn mainly from the middle ranks of senior barristers. However, solicitors are also eligible for the circuit bench if they have served three years as a recorder: they currently number about 60 of the 510 circuit judges.

A recorder is a practising barrister or solicitor who sits as a part-time judge. There are 866 recorders, of whom around 80 are solicitors, who sit for 20 or so days a year in the Crown Court. In addition, there are 385 assistant recorders.

Appointment as a circuit judge, recorder or assistant recorder does not require an invitation from the Lord Chancellor. Any reasonably senior barrister or solicitor can apply to be interviewed and assessed.

The role of the trial judge

A trial judge supervises the conduct of the trial and ensures that the rules are kept; decides any legal issues which arise during the trial, eg concerning the admissibility of evidence; sums up the evidence to the jury, summarising the main factual points covered and guiding the jury on the law; and passes sentence following a plea of guilty by a defendant or a verdict of guilty by a jury.

THE JURY

Jurors are chosen at random from the electoral roll. The qualifications for jury service are contained in the Juries Act 1974. The individual must be:

- registered as a Parliamentary or local government elector
- not less than 18 years old, nor over 65
- have been ordinarily resident in the United Kingdom for a period of at least five years since his or her thirteenth birthday;

and must not be ineligible for or disqualified from jury service. Jurors are summoned to attend at the Crown Court. A failure to attend is punishable as a contempt by a fine. However, a juror may apply to the summoning officer to be excused from his or her obligation where there is good reason. Certain categories are entitled to be excused as of right, eg:

- members of Parliament
- members of the armed services
- members of the medical or psychiatric professions
- people who have served on a jury within the last two years (in some instances, after a long or arduous trial, a judge may excuse members of the jury for life).

The following people fall within the classes of person who are ineligible or disqualified:

ineligible
- past and present members of the judiciary (including justices of the peace: below)
- other people who are or have been within the last ten years concerned with the administration of justice (barristers, solicitors, police officers etc)
- the clergy
- the mentally ill

disqualified
- people who have at any time been detained at Her Majesty's Pleasure, or sentenced to imprisonment or youth custody or detention, for a term of five years or more
- people who within the last ten years have been sentenced to a term of imprisonment, borstal training, youth custody, detention or have been made the subject of a community service order or have been placed on probation within the last five years
- people who are on bail.

Jury challenges
Prosecuting counsel can challenge any juror without putting forward any reason by calling on him or her to 'stand by for the Crown', but this right to challenge is rarely used in practice. Both prosecution and defence can also challenge for cause, ie reject a juror for a particular reason—for example, that the juror is disqualified or ineligible, or is or might be partial.

Jury oath

Each member of the jury is required to swear on oath as follows:

> I will faithfully try the several issues joined between our sovereign lady the Queen and the prisoner at the Bar, and give a true verdict according to the evidence.

MAGISTRATES

There are around 30,000 lay magistrates or 'justices of the peace' (JPs). They undergo special training but are unqualified and not paid. They are ordinary members of the community drawn from a cross-section of society and are chosen for their character, integrity and judgment. They sit on the bench as a form of public service. Magistrates are advised by justices' clerks and, on a day-to-day basis, by other qualified 'legal advisors'. There are also towards 100 stipendiary magistrates who are full-time salaried judges, of equal status to lay magistrates, but who are empowered to sit alone and who, by the nature of their professional expertise, are likely to play a leading role in those areas of the country where they operate—principally London (where they are known as Metropolitan Stipendiary Magistrates) and other large urban centres. The function of a stipendiary is exactly the same as that of a bench of lay magistrates.

Appointment

Lay magistrates are appointed by the Lord Chancellor on behalf of the Sovereign. The Lord Chancellor receives recommendations from local Advisory Committees. Most large cities have an Advisory Committee, whilst other parts of the country are served by committees with responsibility for a county (and posibly divided for the purposes of interviewing and making initial assessments of candidates into Advisory Sub-committees). A special arrangement exists in Greater Manchester, Merseyside and Lancashire, whereby appointments are made by the Chancellor of the Duchy of Lancaster.

There has been a drive to broaden the bench, ie to make it more representative of the community. Another aim is to achieve balance. Committees thus look for applicants from a range of backgrounds and walks of life. They seek nominations by, eg asking local organizations or businesses to encourage suitable people to come forward, and sometimes through notices in the press or in public libraries. Political views are only relevant to prevent benches becoming weighted in any particular direction. However, a survey published in 1995 indicated that a high percentage of magistrates are supporters of the Conservative party, even in some predominantly Labour areas of the country.

Commission of the Peace
Magistrates are appointed to a Commission area and are assigned to a Petty Sessional Division (see *Chapter 2*). They must retire from the bench at 70 years of age when they normally transfer to the supplemental list (as opposed to serving on the active list); and after which they can still carry out a somewhat restricted range of administrative duties.

Training
Before appointment, candidates for the magistracy must give an undertaking to comply with the training requirements. If a magistrate fails to complete an appropriate stage, he or she is expected to resign, unless there is an acceptable explanation. There are highly developed schemes of induction training and basic training for new magistrates, and of obligatory refresher training (ORT) to be completed every three years after the first. All these are compulsory for anyone now joining the bench.

Duties and responsibilities
The main duty of a magistrate is to sit in court on a regular basis. The minimum requirement is 26 sittings a year. Most magistrates sit more than this and senior magistrates may find themselves sitting many more times. Apart from duties in their own PSD, magistrates may be called on to sit elsewhere within the Commission area on occasion, eg where someone closely connected with another bench is charged with an offence. Additionally, magistrates can volunteer to sit in the Crown Court alongside a Judge to hear committals for sentence: *Chapter 3*; and appeals: *Chapter 10*; and to 'sit in' with the judge on jury trials in areas of the country where this practice is adopted.

JUSTICES' CLERKS

Until 1994 justices' clerks were both the chief legal advisors to magistrates and the managers of the courts. They are still the main legal advisors and petty sessional divisions must, in effect, operate under their auspices—but the extent to which an individual justices' clerk manages his or her courts now depends on how changes contained in the Police and Magistrates' Courts Act 1994 have been implemented in a given area. Critical to this will be the way that the arrangements have been forged in relation to the justices' chief executive, who under the 1994 Act is responsible for the day-to-day administration of the courts in an area: below.

At the time of writing, there are 230 justices' clerks in England and Wales (July 1995), generally speaking one for each Petty Sessional Division or group of divisions. They must be barristers or solicitors of at least five years standing (subject to interpretation in accordance with the Courts and Legal Services Act 1990).

Appointment and status

Justices' clerks are appointed by local magistrates' courts committees who must submit one or more names to the Lord Chancellor for approval—the final choice then being restricted to an approved candidate. Reasons must be given if the Lord Chancellor declines to give approval. Approval is also required for removal against the wishes of the local bench—who must also be consulted by the committee in this and a variety of other situations affecting their justices' clerk including on appointment.

A justices' clerk is an office holder, ie of the public office of justices' clerk. His or her employment status depends on whether appointed before or pursuant to the Police and Magistrates' Courts Act 1994. Those appointed before the Act hold office at the pleasure of the magistrates' courts committee—so that, theoretically, a justices' clerk can be removed at will. Those justices' clerks appointed since the Act (and any pre-1994 Act justices' clerks who opt to switch to a contract voluntarily) are '. . . employed by the magistrates' courts committee, on such terms as they may determine' and hold or vacate office in accordance with the terms of a contract of service. Some areas of the country have introduced fixed term contracts—but a proposal which would have made this mandatory failed to survive the passing of the 1994 Act.

For all practical purposes, terms of appointment, employment and pension rights, etc of justices' clerks are analogous to those of government servants. Actual dismissal is rare.

Independence

Given that the lay magistracy is dependent on legal advice provided by the justices' clerk, the role is critical in relation to the doctrine of the separation of powers, ie the separation of state or executive power from independent judicial decision-making: *Chapter 1*. It follows from the essential nature of the lay magistracy that a justices' clerk must be free to carry out his or her responsibilities without outside interference. This principle is enshrined in the 1994 Act, which states that when giving advice to justices in an individual case or when exercising those judicial or quasi-judicial powers conferred on justices' clerks:

> . . . a justices' clerk shall not be subject to the direction of the magistrates' courts committee, the justices' chief executive or any other person.

There is a similar safeguard in relation to other staff.

Duties and responsibilities

The duty of the justices' clerk is to advise magistrates on the law and generally on their powers, either in court or at any other time. There are particular responsibilities relating to evidence, sentencing, procedure and practice. In relation to sentencing, eg a 1990 *Practice Direction* states:

> . . . If it appears to him necessary to do so, or he is requested by the Justices, the Justices' Clerk has the responsibility to . . . advise the Justices generally on the range of penalties which the law allows them to impose and on any guidance relevant to the decisions of the superior courts and other authorities.

In the retiring room

The justices' clerk must advise *on request,* but can also act of his or her *own initiative*—and must do so if the magistrates are plainly about to go wrong in law. He or she may be invited into the magistrates' private retiring room but should not normally go there uninvited. The invitation should only occur where there is a genuine need for legal advice or support. But there is a duty to interrupt magistrates' private deliberations if not to do so could result in error. A modern practice, preferred by many courts, is for advice to be given in open court. This enables the parties to hear what is being said, thus allowing them to make appropriate representations.

Duties in court

Apart from giving legal advice in court, there is a duty to assist unrepresented parties (ie those who have no solicitor or barrister) to put their case. Some proceedings are brought in the name of the clerk to the justices, eg enforcement of fines (they could be brought in the name of the justices' chief executive if this function of a justices' clerk has been passed to him or her by the MCC). There is a duty to take a note of any evidence; or at least of all the main points of the evidence. This will be relied on in the event of a dispute as to what was said by a witness, or if there is an appeal. Magistrates often take their own notes in practice, according to local custom or personal preference (but there is no legal obligation for them to do so).

Judicial and administrative duties

The justices' clerk has certain judicial, or quasi-judicial, powers and duties, eg to grant summonses, adjourn cases, extend bail and to grant legal aid. These have been extended in recent times. By Act of Parliament, justices' clerks must also account to the Exchequer for fines and fees collected; and to victims for compensation paid by offenders. Fines are paid over to the Exchequer via the Lord Chancellor's Department.

JUSTICES' CHIEF EXECUTIVES

Local accountability for the magistrates' courts service is cast on magistrates' courts committees (MCCs) who are made '. . . responsible for the efficient and effective administration of magistrates' courts in their area'. Every magistrates' courts committee must appoint a justices' chief executive to act as clerk to the committee and—'subject to and in accordance with any directions given by the committee'—to carry on the day-to-day administration of the magistrates' courts for the area to which the committee relates. These functions can be discharged via staff employed by the committee. There is a statutory candidate approval scheme similar to that for justices' clerks (above). Candidates must be eligible to be appointed as a justices' clerk. A justices' chief executive can also hold the post of justices' clerk but only if the Lord Chancellor agrees that he or she may hold both appointments and, for a justices' chief executive actually to exercise any of the functions of a justices' clerk, the magistrates' courts committee must specifically authorise this 'generally or in any particular case'.

LAW OFFICERS

The law officers of the Crown are the Attorney General and the Solicitor General. They are appointed from among the senior barrister MPs of the party in power.

Apart from his or her role in the courts, the Attorney General has a political role ie to act as the government's principal legal advisor and answers questions in the House of Commons. He or she is also responsible for the Crown Prosecution Service and the Serious Fraud Office. The national head of the Crown Prosecution Service is the Director of Public Prosecutions, who is in turn responsible to the Attorney General.

CROWN PROSECUTORS

The Crown Prosecution Service (CPS) functions through 12 areas, each headed by a chief Crown prosecutor. In charge locally is a branch Crown prosecutor. Everyday representation in court is usually provided by a Crown prosecutor or senior Crown prosecutor. In court, all are called 'the Crown prosecutor'. The overall national head of the CPS is the Director of Public Prosecutions (DPP) and the responsible Government law officer the Attorney-General (A-G).

Crown prosecutors are usually solicitors, but may be barristers by training. The duty of the prosecutor is to place the facts or evidence before the magistrates in a fair and impartial manner, leaving the court to decide the issues. There is *no* duty to secure a conviction 'at all cost'; or to demand a particular sentence (in contrast eg to the position in American states). Where the police charge a defendant, or in some instances where they are considering a summons, the Crown prosecutor reviews the case and the evidence. There is a duty to take over certain cases from the police and to consider doing so in the case of a private prosecutor, plus a continuing duty—throughout a case—to review the case. Two tests are applied: the evidential sufficiency test; and the public interest test (ie whether prosecution is 'in the public interest'). The case will be discontinued where appropriate.

Solicitors who are in private practice may act as agents for the CPS—just as people may appear for either side in civil cases. CPS agents have only limited authority concerning the conduct of a case.

BARRISTERS AND SOLICITORS

Lawyers are either barristers (also called 'counsel') or solicitors, according to their training. Both have rights of audience in the magistrates' court. Lawyers are known as 'advocates' in court, ie they speak for their client, putting matters forward in the best light. Provided that they do not positively mislead the court, there is no duty to disclose things which are adverse to their client and which have not otherwise emerged.

The kind of advocate regularly seen in magistrates' courts is the local solicitor specialising in criminal and family work. He or she will usually undertake legal aid work (see below). Some solicitors find it cost effective to employ recently qualified barristers for advocacy work. This is a common feature in London and other urban centres where there are barristers' chambers. Sometimes senior barristers, known as Queen's Counsel (or 'silks') appear before magistrates, eg where the client can afford it; or where the case is important or unusually complex. A prosecution by the Health and Safety Executive might eg involve a fatal accident on which a future civil claim in the High Court for substantial damages hinges, or an injury caused on a production line may bring about a need to alter the way items are made by a major manufacturer. Queen's counsel might also be seen in relation to a murder charge or other serious matter at the transfer for trial stage.

The McKenzie friend
A defendant may be aided by what is called a McKenzie friend, ie someone to take notes, quietly make suggestions and give advice. This needs to be authorised by the court and the device can only be used as a means of assisting the defendant and the court, not of hindering the proceedings eg by spinning them out. Courts can hear who they will as an advocate in a given case—a principle established in *O'Toole v Scott* [1965] AC 939. The Courts and Legal Services Act 1991 acknowledges a general right for a court to refuse to hear someone who would normally have rights of audience for reasons which apply to him or her as an individual—but the court must give its reasons.

LEGAL AID

Legal aid is available in relation to proceedings before magistrates' by a variety of routes:

The criminal legal aid scheme
The grant or refusal of criminal legal aid for summary proceedings and, initially, for cases transferred to the Crown Court for trial lies in the hands of the magistrates' court. Either the justices' clerk (or his or her authorised delegate) or the magistrates can grant legal aid. Where the applicant satisfies a means test (below), only magistrates can refuse legal aid, ie under the interests of justice test. There is an appeal against refusal to the Area Committee of the Legal Aid Board which—subject to any fixed fee or franchise arrangements—also assesses the amount of a claim for payment by the solicitor concerned. Legal aid representation in magistrates' courts is normally by solicitor, but a certificate for counsel (ie a barrister) can be authorised, eg in a contentious transfer for

trial for murder where it is desirable that the same lawyer carries the case forward into the Crown Court in the event of its going that far.

There is a twin test for legal aid in criminal proceedings: the interests of justice test (sometimes called 'the Widgery criteria' after Lord Widgery, a former Lord Chief Justice, who initially laid down the principles involved); and a means test. The interests of justice test will only be satisfied if eg personal liberty or reputation is at stake, or where some legal complexity or sensitive issue arises. It might eg be utterly undesirable for the defendant to conduct a personal cross-examination of a child victim of an alleged assault. Legal aid guidelines expand on such matters. Depending on the outcome of the means test, legal aid may be free, or the applicant can be required to pay a 'legal aid contribution order' according to a fixed scale. The applicant is expected to provide evidence of means for the period covering the three months immediately preceding the date of the application.

Duty solicitor schemes at police stations
These provide for assistance to people who have been detained. This form of legal aid is neither means tested nor based on any test concerning the merits of the situation. There are no great formalities, the scheme does not allow or guarantee any choice of solicitor or for continued services by the same solicitor after the defendant is released from police custody or when he or she appears in court.

Duty solicitor schemes at court
Duty solicitor schemes in magistrates' courts provide a 'first aid' service to criminal defendants who arrive at court unrepresented. They are non-means-tested and non-contributory. Duty solicitors can advise defendants in custody; make bail applications; represent defendants in custody who are pleading guilty; give advice to and represent non-custody defendants who, in the duty solicitor's opinion, need such help; and help defendants to apply for legal aid.

The 'green form' scheme
This provides for up to two hours of legal advice and assistance but does not allow for representation at court unless the court specifically extends the form to cover court proceedings. There is a means test which confines the availability of this variety of advice to people with a low disposable income, but there is no test regarding the merits of the case.

The Legal Aid Board
Ultimately, legal aid is administered by the Legal Aid Board under the auspices of the Lord Chancellor. Duty solicitor schemes are funded by the Board, which also deals directly with legal aid in civil cases, with minor exceptions.

WITNESSES

Witness usually attend court voluntarily to give evidence but can be made subject to a witness order (sometimes called a subpoena) or in extreme instances a witness warrant. Witnesses due to appear in the Crown Court are served with a witness order by the magistrates' court at the time of transfer for trial. This may be a full order or a conditional witness order, the latter usually indicating that the particular witness' evidence is unlikely to be disputed and that it will therefore be given by way of the written statement already made and used in the transfer proceedings. Witnesses are later notified of the date when they are required to appear at the Crown Court.

The Crown Court Witness Service operated by Victim Support helps victims of crime, witnesses and their families before, during and after hearing and produces a helpful leaflet entitled 'Going to Court'.

The nature of the evidence which a witness may give is noted in *Chapter 8.*

EXPERTS

Expert witnesses may be called by either the prosecution or the defence to give their opinion on a matter within their own field of expertise. Regular examples are forensic witnesses to give evidence of tests carried out which eg establish a link between the accused person and the crime, medical witnesses to give evidence of injury and engineers to establish the existence, say, of a defect in a motor vehicle or in some other piece of machinery. Contrary to the general rule, expert witnesses are not confined to giving factual evidence provided that in the 'opinion evidence' which they may give is subject to cross-examination in the usual way when they may be called upon to give the reason for their opinion. Sometimes expert witnesses appear for both parties when there may be a conflict of evidence which the court will need to resolve.

The cost of calling an expert witness can be considerable. It is borne by the party calling the witness in the first instance but, assuming that the involvement of the expert was reasonable, it is recoverable by the successful party under the normal rules relating to costs in criminal proceedings, in the case of the defence either from central funds or from the prosecutor.

INTERPRETERS

Increasingly, the need for interpreters is being recognised in a wide range of situations. Interpreters take a special oath to 'truly interpret' the evidence from one language to another, or by sign language to someone with impaired hearing. The task is a highly skilled one given the degree of precision required in legal proceedings, the need to communicate information without adding to, detracting from or adding any judgment or assessment to the witness' evidence. Most courts now have, or have access to, lists of people who are qualified to interpret into and from English and a particular language.

CHAPTER 13

In the Community

THE PROBATION SERVICE

According to a Home Office 'Statement of Purpose' the main responsibilities of the probation service are:

—to provide the courts with advice and information on offenders to assist in sentencing decisions
—to implement community sentences passed by the courts
—to design, provide and promote effective programmes for supervising offenders safely in the community
—to assist prisoners, before and after release, to lead law-abiding lives
—to help communities prevent crime and reduce its effects on victims
—to provide information to the courts on the best interests of children in family disputes
—to work in partnership with other bodies and services in using the most constructive methods of dealing with offenders and defendants.

The document continues by describing the main 'outputs' of the service:

—pre-trial services, including the provision of bail information
—pre-sentence reports for the courts
—the supervision of offenders under community sentences
—reports for the Parole Board and Prison Service
—the supervision of offenders following release from custody
—welfare reports and mediation requested by the courts in children's proceedings.

National and local responsibility

A distinction must be drawn between those matters which are determined nationally, by central government (see under the heading *The Home Office* below), and those dealt with by local 'probation committees' (to be known as a 'probation boards': below) or the chief probation officer for a probation area.

The Home Office

The Home Office has played an increasing role in the development and direction of the probation service. The government's approach is to 'strengthen the local structure' (the Statement of Purpose). The Home Office itself exerts influence in several ways, including:

- by deciding upon and allocating resources for the service. Central government support for all probation services is cash limited, ie the Home Office allocates a finite sum of money and area probation services must then operate within its constraints. Probation areas are financed through local authorities to whom the Home Office pays 80 per cent of current (or revenue) expenditure and, subject to special authorisation, 80 per cent of capital expenditure. In each case, the remaining 20 per cent is funded by the local authority itself (partially accounted for by the revenue support grant). The cost of probation officers in prisons is met by the Prison Service and some hostel costs are funded 100 per cent by the Home Office.
- by producing a statement of purpose and a three year 'rolling plan' alongside which local services must create their own plan. A rolling plan will cover a three year period but is updated annually, thereby providing a medium term view with the opportunity for modification in the light of developing policy or resource implications.
- receiving reports of inspections on a regular basis (see under the heading *Her Majesty's Inspectorate of Probation*, below).

The Probation Service Division (known as 'C6') is part of the Criminal Justice and Constitutional Department of the Home Office and has been instrumental in developing the national standards already adverted to in *Chapter 9*. Various sections of the department deal with such matters as probation hostels (which must be approved centrally), bail information schemes, probation service partnerships and grants to outside organizations, training, competences (ie aspects of probation work at which probation officers and others within the probation service are expected to be competent), non-vocational qualifications (NVQs), staff appraisal, regional in-service training, planning, policy, and the secondment of probation officers to prisons.

Her Majesty's Inspectorate of Probation
A comparatively small, autonomous unit is responsible directly to the Home Secretary for inspecting the work of the probation service and for advising government on related issues. Most probation inspectors are drawn from within the ranks of the probation service. They generally have considerable experience in the probation field, and may have

worked through the grades to reach chief officer level. There is statutory provision allowing suitably qualified people from other professions to become probation inspectors. There are two kinds of inspection:

- *area* inspections, when two or three sections of a probation service's work (eg court reports, community service, sex offenders) are looked at in detail, with sampling exercises and face-to-face discussions between inspectors and probation staff taking place at all levels within the service being inspected. Such inspections are called 'Quality and Effectiveness Inspections' and the final report contains recommendations to the area concerned.
- *thematic* inspections, when a particular area of work is examined eg the preparation of pre-sentence reports or post-custody supervision (ie the supervision of prisoners following their release from prison). A thematic inspection may be carried out in, say, 12 different probation areas and the final report will contain recommendations to the Home Secretary about national issues as well as recommendations to local services. Reports of thematic inspections can also contain recommendations concerning the performance of other agencies within the justice process and government departments with an interest in criminal justice.

As well as recommendations regarding action which needs to be taken to improve standards, Inspectors' reports may also contain 'commendations' whereby government, probation committees and other people can become aware of good work. Reports of both sorts of inspection are open to public scrutiny.

Probation areas and probation committees
At the time of writing, the management of each probation area in England and Wales lies in the hands of a probation committee. However, the government has already paved the way for the creation of 'probation boards'. These boards will carry out a similar function to probation committees, but they will be differently constituted (see below) and—in contrast to the position in relation to probation committees—the chief probation officer for the area will be a full member of the board. Some probation areas have established 'shadow boards' in anticipation of the changeover. The basic responsibilities and functions of committees/boards are broadly comparable: see below.

Probation areas
There are currently 55 probation areas in England and Wales (1995) but this number could be reduced if plans for amalgamation of some of the smaller areas come to fruition.

Probation committees
Each probation area has a probation committee. Traditionally, these committees have comprised representatives from each petty sessional division (PSD) covered by the probation area. There is also usually at least one representative of the local judiciary (generally a circuit judge, ie a judge of the Crown Court). The committee must appoint a chairperson and a deputy from within its membership and may have sub-committees to deal with specific areas of work such as finance or staff matters.

Probation committees have power to co-opt suitably qualified people, eg an academic with a special interest in probation matters, a local councillor or a member of the public with a special interest in criminal justice issues.

Probation boards
As already indicated, probation boards are scheduled to replace probation committees. Their membership will be as follows:

- seven magistrates
- one appointee of the Lord Chancellor
- two appointees of the local authority
- five members of the local community
- the chief probation officer for the area.

Chief probation officers
Every probation area is headed by a chief probation officer (CPO). Until late in 1994 every CPO was from a probation service background and would almost certainly have progressed through the ranks over a number of years. The government has now signalled that it is open to probation committees to appoint CPOs from disciplines other than probation. The first such appointment was made at the end of 1994.

Probation officers
Probation officers make up the vast body of the probation service (often called 'main grade' officers). Their work is likely to include one or more of the following:

- *fieldwork:* attending court, writing pre-sentence reports, supervising offenders
- *probation centre:* running intensive courses for high risk offenders who attend a probation centre
- *group work:* running offender behaviour groups such as programmes for sex offenders, anger management groups, alcohol education courses
- *community service:* supervising non-probation officer staff, attending court, publicising the scheme
- *probation hostels:* managing hostels, selecting and supervising residents, attending court
- *prison work:* working alongside prison officers in the exercise of their welfare function, forging a link with outside supervisors, rehabilitative and pre-release work
- *youth justice:* being a member of an inter-agency youth justice team: see *Chapter 6*
- *bail information:* this is governed by a 'National Standard for Bail Information Schemes' and involves interviewing defendants, verifying information about their circumstances and supplying this information to the CPS.

SOCIAL SERVICES

Local authority social services departments work with many young offenders under the age of 18. Such work is often carried out by members of specialist youth justice teams. Their responsibilities include pre-court diversion work; preparing pre-sentence reports; supervising young offenders subject to supervision orders; providing intermediate treatment schemes, supervised activity programmes, bail support and remand fostering arrangements; and the through-care of young offenders sentenced to custody.

In each local area there is an agreement between the probation service and the social services department over the local division of responsibility for work with offenders aged under 18. In some areas staff operate within their own agencies, while in other areas social workers and probation officers work together in integrated or combined youth justice teams. The degree to which the youth justice policies of social services departments are integrated with their wider policies for children and young people varies: the Social Services Inspectorate has noted that the most effective youth justice services involve single and clearly defined management structures with clear links at all levels with social services departments' wider child care service.

EDUCATION SERVICES

The education service is involved with the criminal justice process in a number of ways, including:

- preparing school reports on pupils appearing before the criminal courts, or alternatively providing relevant information to the agency preparing the pre-sentence report (PSR) for incorporation into that report
- participating in inter-agency groups which co-ordinate local approaches to youth crime and young offenders
- participating in inter-agency panels which make recommendations to the police on the cautioning of young offenders.

MEDICAL AND PSYCHIATRIC SERVICES

The National Health Service, social services departments and the voluntary sector provide a range of facilities for mentally disturbed offenders who are diverted towards appropriate care at the pre-court stage; given probation or supervision orders with a condition of psychiatric treatment; given hospital orders or remanded to hospital; or transferred from prison to hospital. In addition medical services, including the Health Care Service for Prisoners, prepare medical reports on the mental condition of defendants to assist courts in their sentencing decisions.

In a growing number of courts 'duty psychiatrist' schemes and other court psychiatric assessment arrangements have been established: these enable courts to receive speedy medical advice, and in appropriate cases can make arrangements to admit offenders to hospital much more quickly than would otherwise be likely. In 1992 the report of an interdepartmental review of health and social services for mentally disordered offenders (the Reed Committee) recommended an expansion of the number of court assessment schemes, medium secure hospital places and intensive care wards, hostel places and diversion arrangements for mentally disordered offenders and defendants.

THE PRIVATE SECTOR

Private sector involvement in the management of prisons is referred to in *Chapter 14*. The private sector is also involved in the provision of the following services:

- The Court Escort and Custody Service, which is being progressively contracted out throughout England and Wales. By 1997 all court escort services will be provided by the private sector.
- The electronic monitoring (or tagging) of offenders subject to curfew orders began experimentally in three areas in July 1995. The whole electronic monitoring service, ranging from the supply and installation of the equipment to the actual monitoring of those subject to a curfew sentence, is the responsibility of private contractors.

VOLUNTARY ORGANIZATIONS.

The voluntary sector is heavily involved in work with offenders. A wide range of voluntary organizations play a part in this work, ranging from large national bodies such as the National Association for the Care and Resettlement of Offenders (NACRO) to small local organizations managing a single hostel or workshop project. Areas of work in which the voluntary sector is involved include:

Accommodation: providing hostels, shared housing and supported lodgings schemes for ex-offenders.

Employment: providing adult and youth training, work experience, and help and advice on finding employment.

Education: providing offenders with education in basic skills, and information, advice and help on participation in education courses.

Bail: providing accommodation and support for bailed defendants to help avoid unnecessary remands in custody.

Mental health: providing hostels, group homes, day care and advice services for people with a history of mental illness.

Drug/alcohol misuse: providing advice services, residential rehabilitation facilities and day care for people with drug and alcohol problems.

Court-based services: running help desks at courts providing on the spot advice and information to people attending court, as well as 'tea-bars' and refreshment facilities in some instances.

Prisoner's families: providing support, help and advice to the families and friends of people serving prison sentences.

CHAPTER 14

In the Prison System

The role of the Prison Service is summed up in its statement of purpose:

> Her Majesty's Prison Service serves the public by keeping in custody those committed by the courts. Our duty is to look after them with humanity and help them lead law abiding and useful lives in custody and after release.

There are around 130 prison service establishments in England and Wales, including 12 for women. Many of the best known establishments—including Brixton, Manchester (Strangeways), Parkhurst, Pentonville and Wormwood Scrubs—are Victorian. Others are post-war—21 new prisons having been built since 1980—while some are former castles, country houses and military bases.

ORGANIZATION AND STAFFING

The Prison Service became an executive agency in April 1993. Home Office Ministers remain responsible for policy but the Director General of the Prison Service is responsible for the delivery of services. The Prisons Board is the agency's senior management team. Chaired by the Director General, it has six executive directors (the Director of Services, Director of Health Care, Director of Programmes, Director of Custody, Director of Personnel and Director of Finance) and four non-executive Directors from outside the Prison Service.

The management of four prisons is currently contracted out to the private sector and the six new prisons which are currently planned will be designed, built, managed and financed by the private sector.

Each prison is inspected periodically by the Inspectorate of Prisons, which publishes a report of each inspection, carries out thematic inspections on particular aspects of the prison system, and publishes an annual report. Each establishment has its own Board of Visitors, a body of lay people selected by the Home Secretary, which acts as a 'watchdog' overseeing the activities of a prison and the treatment of prisoners.

The Prison Service employs around 39,000 staff, nearly two-thirds of whom are uniformed prison officers while over 1,000 are members of the governor grades. Prison officers with basic internal nursing training are employed as hospital officers in male prisons. Qualified nurses are employed in women's establishments and some are employed in male prisons. Other key staff include:

- medical officers, prison doctors who advise the governor on health matters and prepare reports for courts on prisoners, as well as providing health care;

- probation officers, seconded to the prison, who work alongside prison officers in the exercise of their welfare function, undertake rehabilitative and pre-release work, liaise with prisoners' home probation officers, write reports for the discretionary conditional release process, and advise the prison management team on issues of through-care;

- education officers who run both full time education courses and evening classes; and

- chaplains (Anglican, Catholic and Methodist) who provide opportunities for worship, spiritual counselling and pastoral care, supported by visiting ministers of other denominations and faiths.

PRISONERS—FROM RECEPTION TO RELEASE

Nearly 110,000 people are sent to prison each year. A total of 63,000 people were received into prison as remand prisoners in 1993 whilst 73,000 were received as sentenced prisoners (including many who had previously been remanded in custody and 23,000 for failing to pay a fine). Around 5,000 were also received as civil prisoners, held, for example, under the Immigration Act or for failing to pay maintenance or the community charge. Most remand prisoners (around 60 per cent) are either found not guilty, not proceeded against, given a non-custodial sentence or freed at court.

Reception
From the court, the prisoner will normally be taken to an inner city local prison or remand centre, usually during the evening. The

prisoner will be taken to the reception and be required to shower or bathe, and will then be clothed, fed and given a number and an often brief medical interview before being taken to the wing. (Prisoners may be fingerprinted and, within a day or two, photographed). On leaving reception, prisoners are given a towel, sheets, wash-things, toothbrush and tooth powder.

Local and other closed prisons are divided into a number of wings or halls, often holding different categories of prisoner. Each has a number of levels or landings containing cells. Outside the prisoner's cell is a small metal plate for the prisoner's card, containing number, surname, length of sentence, earliest date of release and religious affiliation.

Women prisoners, remand prisoners and, in some prisons, men serving sentences are allowed to keep their own clothes. Others will be given a denim jacket and trousers, blue and white striped shirt, shoes and two or three pairs of socks, underpants, vests or T shirts, which they can exchange at intervals thereafter. Each prisoner will also be given plastic cutlery, a plate, mug and a pillow case. All prisoners should be allowed to retain some personal possessions at the governor's discretion, including a radio, wristwatch, book, pen and paper. Other possessions will be stored in reception.

During the medical interview the medical officer will assess the prisoner's fitness to work, to remain in prison and whether there is a suicide risk. The suicide rate in prisons is roughly four times the rate for the general population. Young offenders, who are more likely to lack the inner resources to deal with imprisonment, are particularly vulnerable.

Categorisation and allocation
Sentenced adult men (ie aged 21 and over) will initially be held in an observation, classification and allocation unit of a local prison or remand centre, after which they will be placed in a security category, depending on the perceived risk of their escaping and the danger they would pose to the public should this happen.

Sentenced prisoners will either be categorised A (those 'whose escape would be highly dangerous to the public or the police or to the security of the State'), B ('for whom escape must be made very difficult'), C ('cannot be trusted in open conditions' but who 'do not have the will or resources to make a determined escape attempt') or D ('can reasonably be trusted' in open conditions). Unsentenced prisoners are automatically categorised B, unless provisionally placed in Category A. Women and young offenders are categorised simply for open or closed conditions apart from a few women who are categorised as A. Categorisation is reviewed every 12 months and prisoners tend to be moved to less secure conditions as they progress through their sentence.

The prison to which an adult male sentenced prisoner is allocated will depend on his security category, sentence and places available. Many males serving sentences of 18 months or less serve their whole sentence in a local prison. Those serving longer sentences will usually be transferred to a training prison. Category A prisoners will usually be allocated to a dispersal prison, which is a high security closed training prison. Category A women are sent to a separate unit in Durham men's prison. Category D prisoners may be transferred to an open prison. A young offender under sentence will be held in an open or closed young offender institution.

Vulnerable prisoners in need of protection and prisoners perceived as a threat to the maintenance of good order and discipline (GOAD) may be segregated from other prisoners under Rule 43 (Rule 46 in young offender institutions). Vulnerable prisoners generally request segregation, GOAD prisoners are usually segregated against their will. In addition some prisoners needing long-term protection are held in vulnerable prisoner units.

Sentence plans are drawn up for prisoners serving 12 months or more and for all young offenders. These plans aims to ensure that the prisoner's time in custody is spent positively and that problems underlying offending behaviour are tackled. During their sentence many prisoners will join groups or courses which look at problems such as alcohol or drug abuse, gambling, aggression or sexual offending.

Some establishments run treatment programmes for sex offenders which aim to: counter distorted beliefs about relationships; increase awareness of the effects of crimes on victims; get prisoners to accept responsibility for the results of their actions; and enable prisoners to develop ways of preventing a relapse and avoiding high risk situations.

Pre-release
Some prisoners will also go on inmate development and pre-release courses. The courses, usually run by prison officers, cover many topics including housing, work, benefits and rights. Outside agencies, such as citizens advice bureaux, often take part in the courses.

Men serving sentences of six years or more and women serving 18 months or more may be allowed to spend the last six months of their sentence living in a PRES (Pre-release Employment Scheme) hostel either inside or outside the prison. While at the hostel, they will seek regular paid work from which they contribute towards their keep and save for release.

Temporary release
After serving a specified part of their sentence, prisoners can be considered for temporary release to participate in regime-related activities such as community service projects, employment, training or education, and for resettlement purposes towards the end of the prisoner's sentence. However, such opportunities have been substantially reduced following a change in the rules governing temporary release which was announced by the Home Secretary in November 1994.

Release
Prisoners are normally released after breakfast. Property and clothes will be returned to them, and new clothes will be supplied where necessary. Most sentenced prisoners are entitled to a discharge grant intended to cover the prisoner's expenses until he or she can claim benefit.

THE PRISON DAY

The day begins for many prisoners in closed prisons between 7.30 am and 8 am, when cell doors are unlocked and prison officers conduct a roll check to establish that each prisoner is there. Prisoners are counted frequently each day.

Prisoners in cells without access to sanitation at night then queue up to slop out their plastic chamber pots into a communal sluice. (However, the programme to provide decent sanitation in prisons should ensure that slopping out ends by February 1996.) Prisoners then collect hot water for washing and shaving before collecting their breakfast from heated trolleys, which they eat off a tray in their cells.

Between 8.45 am and 9 am, activities begin. Many prisoners will go to work/training or education classes, though some, mainly those in local prisons, may be inactive for much of the day. Prisoners are employed as prison cleaners, kitchen and laundry staff; in farming and gardening activities; in clothing, carpentry and engineering workshops; in assembling components for outside industry—and in sewing mailbags. Prisoners in some open and other training prisons work outside prison with elderly people, with physically and mentally handicapped people and on community projects, but the opportunities for such constructive work have been severely reduced by the recent changes to temporary release arrangements.

Prisoners who are employed currently earn an average of £7 a week. Earnings can be spent in the prison canteen, a small shop which they can usually visit once a week to buy food, tobacco, toiletries, batteries etc. Prisoners who do not have work or classes to go to are paid a flat rate allowance.

During the morning (and, in many establishments, during the afternoon), prisoners in closed establishments exercise outdoors, weather permitting. In many establishments exercise involves walking with other prisoners in a circle in a yard. Prisoners in open prisons do not have exercise periods as such. Juveniles and young adults serving short sentences should have an hour of physical education each weekday. Physical education is very popular with many prisoners. It raises self-esteem, provides a sense of achievement, serves as a means of letting off aggression, and prisoners are allowed a shower afterwards.

After lunch, activities are resumed. Some prisoners will receive visits from family and friends. Some prisons allow visits in the morning. Unconvicted prisoners can normally have visits on at least three days a week, totalling a minimum of one and a half hours and a visit on Saturday or Sunday. Convicted prisoners are normally allowed a minimum of one visit every two weeks. Close relatives on income support or low incomes may get the cost of two visits a month paid by the Home Office.

The final meal of the day in local prisons, tea, is often eaten around eight or nine hours after breakfast, though more prisons have now introduced more flexible meal arrangements. Some prisons allow prisoners to prepare snacks on the wings.

Some prisoners will attend classes during the evening while others will be allowed association, usually by rota. Association may be withdrawn as a punishment or if there are insufficient staff to supervise it. Many prisoners not allowed association will be locked up—often with another prisoner in cells built for one. The typical cell measures perhaps 12 feet by nine by eight. Around 8,700 prisoners were sharing two to a cell in March 1995. This overcrowding is mainly in local prisons and remand centres.

After lock up, lights out. The cell light is turned off from outside.

REQUESTS AND COMPLAINTS

Prisoners wanting to make a request or complaint to the governor are encouraged to discuss their concerns with prison officers to see whether they can be sorted out informally (the majority are). If it is necessary to involve formal procedures, prisoners can submit a request or complaint to the governor: they should normally receive a reasoned reply within seven days. If the problem cannot be resolved within the prison, or if the prisoner wants to appeal against a decision made by the governor, the request, complaint or appeal is forwarded to Prison Service headquarters: the prisoner should receive a reply within six weeks. A prisoner can also petition the Home Secretary or pursue the complaint outside the system at the same time or instead.

A Prisons Ombudsman has been appointed as a final appeal stage for prisoner's grievances: he can make recommendations to the Director General or the Home Secretary.

EARLY RELEASE OF PRISONERS

The Criminal Justice Act 1991 introduced new arrangements for the early release of prisoners and for their supervision and liabilities after release.

Prisoners serving terms of less than four years are released after they have served half their sentences in custody, unless they have been awarded 'additional days' for offences against prison discipline. Long-term prisoners (those serving four years or more) are released (subject to any award of 'additional days') after they have served two-thirds of their sentence. They may be released on licence by the Parole Board between the half-way and two-thirds point of the sentence if the sentence is between four and seven years; if the prisoner is serving seven years or more, the Parole Board can recommend release to the Home Secretary, who makes the final decision.

Prisoners sentenced to a year or more are supervised on release until the three-quarters point of the sentence. Certain sex offenders may be supervised until the end of their sentence if this was ordered by the sentencing court.

Any released prisoner who commits another offence punishable with imprisonment before the end of the original sentence may be liable on conviction to serve the part of the original sentence which was outstanding at the time of the fresh offence as well as any penalty for the new offence.

In the case of prisoners serving discretionary life sentences, imposed for offences other than murder, the Home Secretary is required to release such prisoners after a 'tariff' period—set by the trial judge to reflect the requirements of retribution and deference—if he is so directed by the Parole Board. The Board must be satisfied that the protection of the public does not require the prisoner's further confinement. Where offenders are convicted of murder and receive mandatory life sentences the tariff period is set by the Home Secretary: when it has expired the Home Secretary may release the prisoner if the Parole Board so recommends.

On release, life sentence prisoners remain on licence for the rest of their lives and are subject to recall if their behaviour suggests that they might again be a danger to the public.

THE PAROLE BOARD

The Parole Board comprises a Chairman and over 80 members, six of whom are full-time. Its members include judges, psychiatrists, chief probation officers, criminologists and independent members. It meets in panels of three or four members to consider cases. The Board's role in relation to early release of prisoners is described in *Early release of prisoners*, above.

Part IV

Aspects
of
Criminal Justice

CHAPTER 15

The Royal Commission on Criminal Justice

The establishment of a Royal Commission on Criminal Justice was announced on 14 March 1991 by the then Home Secretary, the Rt Hon Kenneth Baker MP, and the Lord Chancellor, Lord Mackay of Clashfern. The announcement was made on the same day that the Court of Appeal quashed the convictions for murder of the 'Birmingham Six'—the men who had been convicted following bomb explosions in public houses in Birmingham in November 1974, and who had in consequence served over 16 years in prison.

Terms of reference
The terms of reference of the Royal Commission, which was chaired by Viscount Runciman of Doxford, required it:

> to examine the effectiveness of the criminal justice system in England and Wales in securing the conviction of those guilty of criminal offences and the acquittal of those who are innocent, having regard to the efficient use of resources, and in particular to consider whether changes are needed in:
>
> (i) the conduct of police investigations and their supervision by senior police officers, and in particular the degree of control that is exercised by those officers over the conduct of the investigation and the gathering and preparation of evidence;
>
> (ii) the role of the prosecutor in supervising the gathering of evidence and deciding whether to proceed with a case, and the arrangements for the disclosure of material, including unused material, to the defence;
>
> (iii) the role of experts in criminal proceedings, their responsibilities to the court, prosecution and defence, and the relationship between the forensic science services and the police;
>
> (iv) the arrangements for the defence of accused persons, access to legal advice, and access to expert evidence;
>
> (v) the opportunities available for an accused person to state his position on the matters charged and the extent to which the courts might draw proper inferences from primary facts, the conduct of the

accused, and any failure on his part to take advantage of an opportunity to state his position;

(vi) the powers of the courts in directing proceedings, the possibility of their having an investigative role both before and during the trial, and the role of pre-trial reviews; the courts' duty in considering evidence, including uncorroborated confession evidence;

(vii) the role of the Court of Appeal in considering new evidence on appeal, including directing the investigation of allegations;

(viii) the arrangements for considering and investigating allegations of miscarriages of justice when appeal rights have been exhausted;

and to make recommendations.

Proposals

The Royal Commission held 43 meetings and signed its report on 2 June 1993. The report, containing 352 recommendations for change, was published on 6 July 1993. Speaking on the occasion of its publication, Viscount Runciman said:

I am confident that our recommendations, if implemented as a whole, will significantly reduce the risk of innocent people being convicted and the guilty walking free.

The main proposals of the Royal Commission included the following:

Miscarriages of justice

• A new independent review authority, called the Criminal Cases Review Authority, should be set up to consider allegations of miscarriage of justice, to supervise investigations of such allegations where necessary, and to refer appropriate cases to the Court of Appeal.

• The new authority should consist of both lay and lawyer members and be staffed by lawyers and administrators, with direct access to specialist advisers.

Ethnic minorities

• Research and monitoring should be carried out in the areas of potential discrimination against members of minority ethnic groups.

140

• Judges should be able in exceptional cases to order the selection of a jury containing up to three people from ethnic minority communities.

Police investigations

• The police should have the power to take saliva samples from suspects in order to identify offenders through DNA profiling.

• A national data bank should be set up to contain samples from all those convicted of serious criminal offences.

• New national training in basic interviewing skills should be given to all police officers.

• All forces should put in place a 'helpline' scheme under which officers can report their concerns about possible malpractice.

Conditional police bail

• The police should be empowered to impose conditions on defendants when releasing them on police bail.

Safeguards for suspects

• Neither the judge nor prosecution counsel should be allowed to comment adversely at trial on a suspect's silence in police custody.

• Continuous video recording of police custody suites should be brought in.

• A judicial warning should be given to the jury in cases where confession evidence is involved.

Committal and mode of trial

• Committal hearings in magistrates' courts should be abolished.

• Defendants should lose the right to insist on trial by jury for offences triable either way. Where the defendant and the prosecution disagree on where a case should be tried, the decision should be taken by the magistrates in accordance with statutory criteria.

Disclosure

• Defendants who intend to advance a defence must disclose the substance of their defence in advance of the trial or risk adverse comment being made in front of the jury.

• The prosecution's initial duty should be to supply the defence with copies of all material relevant to the offence or to the offender or to the surrounding circumstances of the case, whether or not the prosecution intend to rely on that material. Requests for further disclosure by the defence should be on the basis of likely relevance to the line of defence disclosed.

• The prosecution should be able to apply for a ruling of the court on the non-disclosure of sensitive material which may not be covered by public interest immunity.

Pre-trial procedures

• New pre-trial procedures to assist in clarifying and defining the issues in the case before trial should be set out in practice directions and rules of court.

Trials

• The rules on corroboration should be abolished and, when a warning from the judge is required, this should be tailored to the particular circumstances of the case.

Sentence discounts

• There should be a more open system of sentence discounts, with earlier pleas attracting higher discounts.

• At the defendant's request judges should be able to give an indication of the sentence if the defendant were to plead guilty.

Forensic science

• A Forensic Science Advisory Council should be created to oversee the standards and provision of forensic science services, including progress on a code of practice covering professional ethics and duties of disclosure.

Court of Appeal

• The Court of Appeal should be more prepared to overturn verdicts which it believes are or may be unsafe and to order retrials where practicable.

• The Court of Appeal should be more prepared to receive fresh evidence and to accept alleged errors by trial lawyers as a ground of appeal.

• Senior circuit judges nominated by the Lord Chief Justice should be able to sit as members of the Court of Appeal.

The 1994 Act
A number of the Royal Commission's proposals were implemented in the Criminal Justice and Public Order Act 1994. For example, the Act:

•Redefined saliva and mouth swabs as 'non-intimate' samples and extended to all recordable offences the power to take non-intimate samples without consent.

• Empowered the police to impose conditions on defendants released on police bail after being charged with an offence.

• Abolished the committal for trial procedure and replaced it by a new 'transfer for trial' procedure which does not involve oral advocacy for represented defendants except in limited cases.

• Required courts to take into account the timing and circumstances of a guilty plea and, if this leads to a less severe sentence, to state this in open court.

• Provided that the court need not be warned about the dangers of convicting on the uncorroborated evidence of a co-accused, nor in sexual cases on the uncorroborated evidence of the victim; and that various sexual offences hitherto requiring corroboration should no longer require it.

• Provided that circuit judges who are approved for the purpose by the Lord Chancellor may be asked to sit in the Court of Appeal (Criminal Division) to hear appeals or applications for leave to appeal.

However, the Government rejected the recommendation of the Royal Commission that the status quo should be maintained in relation to the 'right of silence' (ie the rule that no inferences could be drawn from a defendant's silence at various points during the investigation process). Instead, the 1994 Act provided that, when a defendant questioned under caution has not mentioned a fact that he could reasonably have mentioned, such inferences as appear proper can be drawn during trial, transfer or during a determination of whether there is a case to answer. It also provided that if the defendant elects not to give evidence at the trial, it is open to the court or jury to draw such inferences as appear proper from the failure to give evidence.

Subsequent developments

The Criminal Appeal Bill, published in February 1995, implements a key recommendation of the Royal Commission by establishing a Criminal Cases Review Commission to investigate possible miscarriages of justice. The proposals contained in the Bill follow those set out in a discussion paper issued by the Home Office in March 1994 entitled 'Criminal Appeals and the Establishment of a Criminal Cases Review Commission'. The Commission will direct and supervise investigations into possible miscarriages of justice arising from convictions in magistrates' courts and Crown Courts in England, Wales and Northern Ireland. The Bill also amends the statutory provisions relating to appeals against conviction to the Court of Appeal.

In May 1995 the Home Secretary published a consultation paper entitled 'Disclosure', which builds on the approach proposed by the Royal Commission. The main proposals in the consultation paper would require:

- the investigator to preserve any material gathered or generated during the criminal investigation which led to the charges against the defendant, and make it available to the prosecutor;

- the prosecution to provide the defence with material on which it intends to rely, and material which it does not intend to rely on but which might undermine the prosecution case;

- the defence to provide sufficient details of its case to identify the issues in dispute. This would enable the prosecution to assess whether it had any additional undisclosed material which was relevant to that case, and which the prosecution would then disclose.

An adverse inference could be drawn at the trial if the defendant refused to comply, for example by not disclosing the details of his or her case.

CHAPTER 16

Protection from Discrimination

Section 95 Criminal Justice Act 1991 requires the Home Secretary to publish information each year for the purpose of facilitating the performance by persons engaged in the administration of criminal justice of 'their duty to avoid discrimination against any persons on the ground of race or sex or any other improper ground'. This provision applies to all people engaged in the criminal justice process, whether as judges, magistrates, administrators, police, Crown prosecutors, probation officers, social workers and so on.

The evidence which has given rise to concern about the possible discriminatory effects of decision making in the criminal justice system is summarised in *Chapter 6* of *Criminal Justice in Transition* (Waterside Press, 1994).

Booklets published by the Home Secretary in pursuance of his statutory duty under section 95 include 'Race and the Criminal Justice System' (1992), 'Gender and the Criminal Justice System' (1992), 'Digest: Information on the Criminal Justice System in England and Wales' (1993) and 'Race and the Criminal Justice System' (1994).

Ethnic Monitoring
Since the Criminal Justice Act 1991 each of the criminal justice agencies has taken steps to guard against discrimination and the momentum is growing steadily. The aim is to put in place a monitoring system which will make it possible to track a defendant's progress through the criminal justice system:

• The police started monitoring stops and searches in 1993 and consideration has been given to extending this monitoring to other activities (eg arrests and disposals).

• In 1993 the Crown Prosecution Service initiated a monitoring system designed to assess the number of cases identified by the police as containing an element of racial motivation and to review decisions taken by Crown prosecutors. However, the data from the monitoring survey proved disappointing when analysed and the CPS is therefore examining alternative measures including research work to help assess the effectiveness of racial attacks policies and initiatives in dealing with cases referred to the CPS.

• A pilot project has been initiated at Leicester magistrates' court to test the procedures for gathering information on the ethnic origin of defendants appearing before the courts in order to monitor bail and sentencing. It is hoped that the lessons learned will assist in setting up systems of ethnic monitoring in all the courts in England and Wales.

• A national system for race and ethnic monitoring was introduced in the probation service in 1992. It currently extends to pre-sentence reports, probation, community service and combination orders, through-care cases and bail information schemes.

• The Prison Service introduced new ethnic codes for monitoring in 1992 to ensure consistency with other agencies.

Policy and practice
Examples of initiatives in the areas of policy or practice include:

• The Lord Chancellor's Department and the Home Office have issued guidance to courts, requiring them to develop policies and working practices to ensure equality of treatment for people of all races. The Judicial Studies Board has established an Ethnic Minorities Advisory Committee. Its initial chairman, Mr Justice Brooke, adopted a prominent role in speaking to judges and magistrates, and in the public arena, about the need to improve the way the courts deal with people from ethnic minorities. Since the Ethnic Minorities Advisory Committee was set up in 1991, all the Board's residential training courses have included sessions on issues concerning ethnic minorities. Training has covered Crown Court judges, recorders, assistant recorders and stipendiary magistrates, and a training pack has been developed for new lay magistrates.

• The Law Society and the Bar have established Race Relations Committees. The Law Society has a code of practice on racial discrimination governing service delivery, acceptance of instructions, instructions to barristers and employment matters. The Bar Council has adopted a detailed race equality policy, which it intends should result in at least 5 per cent of members of each chambers being drawn from minority ethnic groups.

• The professional organizations involved in the probation service have taken steps to promote racial equality in every aspect of the service's work, including the production of policy statements and practice guidance. Area probation services have produced equal opportunities policy statements, given special responsibility for race relations to staff members of chief officer grade, and introduced monitoring of the service's court reports and other areas of practice to ensure that they are non-discriminatory.

• In 1993 the Association of Chief Police Officers and the Commission for Racial Equality issued a practical guide to all forces entitled 'Policing and Racial Equality'. Police forces have adopted equal opportunities policies and have taken a range of initiatives to increase the recruitment of staff from minority ethnic groups and to develop training on race issues.

• The Crown Prosecution Service has adopted a policy statement on race relations and a programme for action on race containing a wide range of measures to ensure equality of treatment for staff from minority ethnic groups. It has included racial motivation in the code for Crown prosecutors as one of the factors to be considered when assessing whether prosecution is required in the public interest.

• The prison service has developed a particularly comprehensive race relations policy. In individual prisons race relations liaison officers have been appointed and race relations management teams established to implement the policies of the service. A race relations manual was launched in 1991 setting out detailed policies on monitoring, access to facilities, work, education and training, allocation of accommodation, religion, diet, discipline matters, racially derogatory language, complaints of racial discrimination, and contacts with ethnic minority organizations outside prison. Training on race issues has been reviewed and updated throughout the prison service. An offence of racially discriminatory behaviour is now included in the prison staff disciplinary code.

• The Justice' Clerks' Society has published a wide-ranging document designed to promote equality entitled 'Dealing with Disadvantage' and set up a working group on 'Black People in Magistrates' Courts'.

• The Home Office is providing funding for a three year NACRO project which is aimed at helping local criminal justice agencies to gain the confidence of local minority ethnic communities. The project provides information and advice to criminal justice agencies, helps them to improve service delivery, and assists in the implementation of non-discriminatory policies.

• In 1994 the government reconvened the interdepartmental Racial Attacks Group, which aims to promote greater co-operation between the police and other agencies in preventing and dealing with racial attacks. Since 1993 national police performance indicators have included action taken in response to racial incidents.

CHAPTER 17

Multi-Agency Working

Although the various services of the criminal justice system are independent, they do not act in isolation. Operational and policy decisions by one service can affect the workload, output and resource requirements of others. Effective co-operation within the system is crucial to its efficient management and performance.

Close contact between government departments is maintained at ministerial level and by officials of the Home Office, the Lord Chancellor's Department and the Crown Prosecution Service. Examples of liaison include:

• the establishment of the 'Pre-Trial Issues Working Group' to consider ways in which the working practices and procedures associated with bringing cases to court could be improved. It has published a large number of recommendations designed to achieve this aim which are in the process of being implemented.

• inter-departmental work which currently covers issues such as the retention of business at magistrates' courts which does not require Crown Court jurisdiction; initiatives to improve value for money in the criminal justice system; the tackling of race issues throughout the criminal justice process, including the introduction of ethnic monitoring; and recommendations from the Royal Commission on Criminal Justice.

• streamlining of information exchange between criminal justice services and departments through 'Co-ordination of Computerisation in the Criminal Justice System' (CCCJS).

CRIMINAL JUSTICE CONSULTATIVE COUNCIL

Co-ordination within the criminal justice system has been enhanced by the setting up in 1992 of the Criminal Justice Consultative Council and 24 area criminal justice liaison committees, following a recommendation of Lord Woolf in his report on prison disturbances in 1991. The membership of these committees includes senior representatives of the police, probation service, Crown Prosecution Service, prison service, judges, magistrates and the legal profession. Both the Consultative Council and area committees are chaired by the judiciary. Their purpose is to promote better understanding, co-operation and co-ordination in the administration of the criminal justice system.

Lord Justice Rose is the current Chairman of the Criminal Justice Consultative Council. Its membership includes Permanent Secretaries from the Home Office, the Department of Health and the Lord Chancellor's Department, a Chief Probation Officer, a Chief Constable, a senior solicitor and barrister, the Chairman of the Magistrates' Association, a circuit judge, a justices' clerk and a Director of Social Services.

Area committees are chaired by a resident judge. The membership includes the circuit administrator from the Crown Court, a chief probation officer, chief constable, chief Crown prosecutor, a justices' clerk, a chairman of a magistrates' bench, a barrister and solicitor, a director of social services, and either the prison service area manager or a governor of a local prison. The committees have the responsibility of promoting better understanding, co-operation and co-ordination in the criminal justice system by in particular:

- exchanging information and giving advance notice of local developments which may affect other parts of the system
- formulating co-ordinated area priorities, strategies and plans to give effect to national and locally agreed policies
- considering problems and issues raised by services and court user committees and developing solutions which can be implemented throughout the area
- considering issues and proposals from the Criminal Justice Consultative Council and raising issues with the Council or with government departments which seem to require a national solution
- promoting the spread of good practice.

USER GROUPS

Liaison groups—usually called 'user groups'—comprising the main participants in the criminal justice process at local level exist in relation to most magistrates' courts (see *Chapter 2*) and at each Crown Court centre (see *Chapter 3*).

PARTNERSHIP

'Partnership' is a word which has been used increasingly in recent years in discussions about the improvement of the services delivered by public service organizations. In the criminal justice process, agencies have increasingly been required to think of themselves as part of a co-ordinated network, and to give active consideration to working in collaboration with other agencies to create a cohesive framework for responding to crime. Among the developments which have required such collaboration are new arrangements for sentence planning and through-care for prisoners, which involve close collaboration between the prison and probation services. Both services have jointly produced a national through-care framework document (the 'National Framework for the Through-care of Offenders in Custody to the Completion of Supervision in the Community'). The new arrangements are underpinned locally by contracts consisting of a through-care business plan and a three year through-care development plan agreed between chief probation officers and prison governors.

The Criminal Justice Act 1991, together with a change to the Probation Rules made in 1994, gave probation committees a power to make grants to voluntary and private sector organizations for partnership work. In a decision document 'Partnership in Dealing with Offenders in the Community' (1992) the Home Office set out the government's decisions on partnership between probation services and the independent sector (ie voluntary and private sector organisations) in dealing with offenders in the community. The decisions included:

- an expectation that each probation area should expect to spend a minimum of around 5 per cent of its total revenue budget on partnership work run by the independent sector
- the establishment of a National Partnership Forum to develop national guidance, monitor the development of partnership and arrangements, and make recommendations on the 'core' funding of voluntary organizations at national level

• the submission by each probation service of a local partnership plan for approval nationally
• the establishment of local strategy groups including representatives of the independent sector to be responsible for the development of agreed plans for dealing with offenders in the community, including plans for local funding of independent sector organizations.

A National Partnership Forum was established in 1992 and guidance on the development of partnership plans, drawn up in consultation with the Forum, was issued to probation services in December 1993. Probation services were required to submit local partnership plans for the three year period 1994 to 1997.

CHAPTER 18

Victims of Crime

In 1990, the government published a *Victim's Charter*. This outlined the rights of victims and set out the way in which victims should be treated by the various agencies. In consequence, there have been improvements in the support given to victims of crime and more sensitive treatment. For example, the Crown Prosecution Service has produced guidelines for staff on the treatment of witnesses and victims.

The criminal justice services have also made a number of moves to improve the extent to which victims are kept informed of the progress of a case and given the opportunity in serious cases to provide relevant information to be taken into account by those taking decisions in such areas as prosecution, bail, parole and home leave.

VICTIM SUPPORT

A National Association of Victim Support Schemes (NAVSS)—now simply 'Victim Support'—was formed in 1979. There are local support schemes throughout most of England and Wales. The aim is to provide a comprehensive service for victims of crime, to raise awareness of the effects of crime and to work for changes which will assist victims. The number of referrals has grown to around one million per year. There are nearly 8000 volunteers and about 700 full-time employees. The government makes a grant to Victim Support, amounting to more than £9 million pounds in 1994/95.

Victim support schemes have a co-ordinator and a team of trained volunteers. The police give details of victims to the local victim support scheme, which then contacts them with the offer of help and advice. They counsel victims and provide practical help ranging from assistance on household security to making insurance claims and applying to the Criminal Injuries Compensation Scheme (see below).

Victim Support also manages witness services in Crown Courts: these are financed by the Home Office and supported by the Lord Chancellor's Department. Each court has a co-ordinator with a team of specially selected volunteers, trained to give practical and emotional

154

support to victims of crime and other vulnerable witnesses attending court.

LEGAL REMEDIES

There are various ways in which victims can be compensated or have their property reinstated. A victim of crime can sue in the civil courts (usually for 'tort', the name given to a civil wrong). Awards are also made by the Criminal Injuries Compensation Scheme in cases of violent crime. As a general principle, an accused cannot recover twice over, but eg proof of a conviction goes a considerable way to reinforce a civil claim if, for good and explicit reasons, the criminal court has declined to make an award.

COMPENSATION ORDERS

Reparation is a central object of sentencing and courts are encouraged to award compensation whenever possible. This is enhanced by statutory provisions and the current climate in which the position of victims is constantly highlighted.

Priority
Where both a fine and compensation are considered appropriate, but the offender's means are not adequate to pay both in full, the court is required to give preference to a compensation order. It would therefore be wrong to reduce the amount of compensation because of the defendant's means and then impose a fine as well. Thus, compensation may be the *only* sentence for the offence. It may also be *in addition* to any other sentence (when it is called an 'ancillary order').

Compensation must be considered
Where an offence causes loss, damage or personal injury, the court is obliged by law to consider whether the offender should pay compensation to the victim or for the victim's benefit. Personal injury includes both physical or mental injury. An award can thus be made not only eg for a cut or fracture, but for terror, distress or inconvenience caused by the offence.

In the Crown Court the amount of a compensation order is unlimited. Magistrates are limited to £5000 per offence. The court can also order the defendant to pay compensation for loss, damage or injury caused by offences which it has been asked to take into

155

consideration (TICs), as well as those in respect of which it has actually convicted the defendant. Here, the total is limited to the maximum it could order for the offences of which the accused is convicted.

Application

Generally speaking, an application is made by prosecuting counsel or the CPS. But this is not essential and the victim does not need to apply to the court, or request anyone to do so on his or her behalf. The court has power to make an award of its own motion and without a specific application—always, in the end result, provided that sufficient information is forthcoming to enable the court to fix the amount of the award.

When a court is considering making a compensation order, it must satisfy itself that actual loss, damage or injury has resulted from the offence which the offender has committed (of which he or she has been convicted or has asked to be taken into consideration).

The court will look at the cost of replacement or repair of goods damaged. Where the items are of sentimental value it may be possible to draw common-sense comparisons with other property losses and the likely effect on the victim.

A court will also consider loss of earnings following time off work due to an attack on the person of the victim. It will also look at more intangible matters such as pain and suffering and any loss of facility.

Often the prosecutor and the offender will agree the amount of compensation that can be ordered by the court. Where there is any real issue as to the offender's liability to pay compensation the court will normally hear evidence presented by the prosecutor who may decide to call the victim to give evidence or prove the loss, damage or injury by other evidence such as a receipt or a medical report. The offender may then make representations and call evidence.

The amount need not be proved to the same extent as other matters in criminal cases need to be, but there must be some evidential basis on which the court can arrive at a figure.

Financial circumstances of the offender

Once the court is satisfied that there has been injury, loss or damage of a certain value, its next obligation is to consider the offender's financial circumstances. It is obliged to have regard to his or her means so far as they appear or are known to the court. The Court of Appeal has interpreted this to mean that a compensation order should be such as to enable the offender to complete payment within a reasonable time.

This will normally be within 12 months but can be extended to up to three years where circumstances justify this.

Reasons
The court must give reasons if it decides *not* to make an order for compensation where there has been loss, damage or personal injury to someone. These reasons must be announced in open court and recorded by the court.

RESTITUTION

Where goods have been stolen and a person is convicted of an offence relating to the theft, the court may order the restoration of the goods to the person entitled to recover them (or of other goods bought with the proceeds of realisation). A restitution order can also be made against a defendant following a conviction for dishonest handling of goods, obtaining property by deception or blackmail. Goods include all kinds of property except land. An order can be made in respect of offences taken into consideration (TICs).

Restitution orders can be made by the court of its own volition or on application. A restitution order takes one of three forms, ie an order that:

- anyone having possession or control of the goods restore them to a person entitled to them; or
- any other goods directly or indirectly representing the original stolen goods be delivered by the convicted person to the applicant entitled to them; or
- any money found on the convicted person not exceeding the value of the stolen goods be paid to the person entitled to them.

In appropriate circumstances a court may make orders for both restitution and compensation eg if property is recovered but damaged.

CRIMINAL INJURIES COMPENSATION

The Criminal Injuries Compensation Scheme, established in 1964, provides financial compensation to the victims of crimes of violence and to those injured in attempting to apprehend offenders or prevent crime. The minimum award by the scheme is currently £1,000 and injuries meriting lower awards cannot be compensated by the scheme. At the time of writing (July 1995) the government is taking through Parliament a Criminal Injuries Compensation Bill, which will replace the present scheme with a new 'tariff-based' system. This follows an earlier attempt by the government to alter the scheme without legislation in 1994, which was declared illegal by the courts.

The original version of the scheme assessed awards on the basis of common law damages—ie the amount which would be awarded in the civil courts if the victim sued his or her attacker. Awards were assessed by members of the Criminal Injuries Compensation Board, which comprised lawyers chosen for their expertise in the field of personal injury legislation. Awards consisted of:

- compensation for the pain and suffering experienced by the victim as a result of injury, and
- financial loss such as past and future loss of earnings (up to a maximum of one and a half times average industrial earnings), non-recoverable medical expenses or costs of aids to disabled living and adaptations to the home of someone rendered disabled.

The scheme sought to reflect the losses actually sustained by the individual victim.

Under the new scheme, payments will be based on a 'tariff' whereby injuries will be classified into 25 bands ranging from £1,000 (eg for an undisplaced nasal fracture) to £250,000 (for paralysis of all four limbs or permanent extremely serious brain damage). Injuries of similar severity will be grouped together in a band and cases within each band will attract the same lump sum payment. As a result of widespread criticism of the 1994 version of the government's tariff scheme, in May 1995 it was announced that a number of additional features would be incorporated in the scheme, including the following:

- In addition to the tariff payment, those who are incapacitated for 28 weeks or more will be entitled to a separate payment for loss of earnings or potential earnings (subject to a cap of one and a half times the national average industrial wage).

- In cases of incapacity for 28 weeks or more there will also be payment for special care costs: these could include, for

158

example, home mobility and fittings, special wheelchairs, fees for care in a nursing home etc.

• In fatal cases a fixed payment will be made to each qualifying beneficiary in addition to payment to cover reasonable funeral expenses. There will also be payment in appropriate cases for dependency or loss of support (capped at one and a half times the national average industrial wage).

• Special provision will be made to enable victims who receive awards of more than £50,000 to purchase annuities, thus providing a guaranteed, index-linked, tax free income.

Awards will be subject to an overall limit on any individual award of £500,000. If a claimant is dissatisfied with an award, he or she will be able to ask for a review of the decision. This will be carried out by a staff member of a higher grade than the one who made the original decision. If the claimant then wishes to contest the result of the review, he or she may apply for a hearing by an independent appeal panel, which will have as its members a mixture of lawyers, doctors and others with relevant experience.

THE RIGHTS OF VICTIMS

In February 1995 Victim Support published a statement entitled 'The Rights of Victims of Crime—A Call for Action', together with a policy paper entitled 'The Rights of Victims of Crime'. The statement began:

> In modern times, the state has rightly taken over from victims the duty of prosecuting offenders and dealing with them if convicted. Victim Support believes that victims should therefore have a right to certain standards of treatment—not merely out of concern for their welfare, but because it is in the interests of society as a whole.

It argued that victims should have the right:

• to be free of the burden of decisions relating to the offender
• to receive information and explanation about the progress of the case, and to have the opportunity to provide their own information about the case for use in the criminal justice process
• to be protected in any way necessary
• to receive compensation

- to receive respect, recognition and support.

The policy paper observed that the Victim's Charter of 1990:

> ... was a major landmark in the development of policies for victims of crime, as it confirmed for the first time that there is a problem to be addressed. Many important achievements have followed. There are, however, some fundamental questions which remain unanswered, and many improvements, agreed at policy level, whose implementation in practice has been slow, mainly because of the low priority which is still accorded to victim issues amongst the other demands of criminal justice.

One of the touchstones for progress in criminal justice between now and the end of the century will be the extent to which agencies can continue to improve their treatment of victims and recognition of victims' rights, in ways which are consistent with fairness, proper safeguards and justice for those accused and convicted of criminal offences.

Appendix: Criminal Justice Organizations

Government Departments

Home Office, 50 Queen Anne's Gate, London SW1H 9AT, Tel: 0171 273 3000

Lord Chancellor's Department, Trevelyan House, 30 Great Peter Street, London SW1P 2BY, Tel: 0171 210 8562

Department of Health, Wellington House, 135 - 155 Waterloo Road, London SE1 8UG, Tel: 0171 972 2000

Courts

Magistrates' Association, 28 Fitzroy Square, London W1P 6DD, Tel: 0171 387 2353

Justices' Clerks' Society, The Law Courts, Petters Way, Yeovil, Somerset, BA20 1SW, Tel: 01935 34159

Judicial Studies Board, 14 Little St James's Street, London SW1A lDP, Tel: 0171 925 0185

Legal Profession

General Council of the Bar, 3 Bedford Row, London WC1R 4DB, Tel: 0171 242 0082

Law Society, 113 Chancery Lane, London WC2A 1PL, Tel: 0171 320 5812

Society of Black Lawyers, Unit 314, Brixton Enterprise Centre, 444 Brixton Road, London SW9 8EJ, Tel: 0171 274 4000 ext 346

Prosecution

Crown Prosecution Service, 50 Ludgate Hill, London EC4M 7EX, Tel 0171 273 8000

Serious Fraud Office, Elm House, 10/16 Elm Street, London, WC1X OBJ, Tel: 0171 239 7272

Police

Association of Chief Police Officers, Room 311, Wellington House, Buckingham Gate, London SW1E 6BE, Tel: 0171 230 7184

Police Superintendents' Association, 67a Reading Road, Pangbourne, Berkshire RG8 7JD, Tel: 01734 844055

Police Federation, 15 Langley Road, Surbiton, Surrey KT6 6LP, Tel: 0181 399 2224

Prisons

H M Prison Service, Cleland House, Page Street, London, SW1P 4LN Tel: 0171 217 3000

Prison Governors' Association, Room 409, Horseferry House, Dean Ryle Street, London SW1P 2AW, Tel: 0171 217 8591

Prison Officers' Association, Cronin House, 245 Church Street, London N9 9HW, Tel: 0181 803 0255

Association of Members of Boards of Visitors, Secretary: Juliet Cavill JP, 68 The Causeway, Coalpit Heath, Bristol, Avon BS17 2PG

National Association for Prison Visitors, 46B Hartington Street, Bedford MK41 7RL, Tel: 01234 359763

Prisoners' Advice Service, 57 Chalton Street, London NW1 1HU, Tel: 0171 388 5886

Women in Prison, 3b Aberdeen Studios, 22 Highbury Grove, London N5 2EA, Tel: 0171 226 5879

Black Female Prisoners' Scheme, Eurolink Business Centre, 49 Effra Road, London SW2 1BZ, Tel: 0171 733 5520

Parole

Parole Board, Abell House, John Islip Street, London SW1P 4LH, Tel: 0171 217 5314

Probation

Association of Chief Officers of Probation, 212 Whitechapel Road, London E1 1BJ, Tel: 0171 377 9141

National Association of Probation Officers, 3-4 Chivalry Road, London SW11 1HT, Tel: 0171 223 4887

Central Probation Council, 38 Belgrave Square, London SW1X 9NT, Tel: 0171 245 9480

Association of Black Probation Officers, 7 Canadian Avenue, London SE6 3AU

National Association of Asian Probation Staff, c/o Rashid Gumra, Probation Office, 53 Billing Road, Northampton NN1 SDB Tel: 01604 35274

Resettlement of offenders

National Association for the Care and Resettlement of Offenders, 169 Clapham Road, London SW9 OPU Tel: 0171 582 6500

Apex Trust, St Alphage House, Wingate Annexe, 2 Fore Street, London EC2Y 5DA, Tel: 0171 638 5931

Bourne Trust, Lincoln House, 1-3 Brixton Road, London SW9 6DE, Tel: 0171 582 1313

New Bridge, 27a Medway Street, London SW1P 2BD, Tel: 0171 976 0779

Society of Voluntary Associates, 350 Kennington Road, London SE11 4LH, Tel: 0171 793 0404

Prisoners' families

Federation of Prisoners' Families Support Groups, Cambridge House, Cambridge Grove, London W6 OLE, Tel: 0181 741 4578

Victims

Criminal Injuries Compensation Authority, Tay House, 300 Bath Street, Glasgow G2 4JR, Tel: 0141 331 2726

Victim Support, Cranmer House, 39 Brixton Road, London SW9 6DZ, Tel: 0171 735 9166

Support After Murder and Manslaughter, Cranmer House, 39 Brixton Road, London SW9 6DZ, Tel: 0171 735 3838

Childline, Freepost 1111, London N1 0BR, Tel: 0800 1111

Women's Aid Federation, P O Box 391, Bristol BS99 7WS, Tel: 0117 963 3494

Mediation

Mediation UK, 82a Gloucester Road, Bristol, BS7 8BN, Tel: 0117 924 1234

Reform

Penal Affairs Consortium, 169 Clapham Road, London, SW9 0PU, Tel: 0171 582 6500

Howard League for Penal Reform, 708 Holloway Road, London N19 3NL, Tel: 0171 281 7722

Prison Reform Trust, 2nd Floor, The Old Trading House, 15 Northburgh Street, London EC1V 0AH, Tel: 0171 251 5070

Justice, 59 Carter Lane, London EC4V 5AQ, Tel: 0171 329 5100

Youth justice

National Association for Youth Justice, c/o Ken Hunnybun, 193 Markfield Road, Groby, Leicestershire LE6 0FT

Other

Institute for the Study and Treatment of Delinquency, King's College, Strand, London WC2R 2LS, Tel: 0171 873 2822

Index

Further introductory books from Waterside Press

Introduction to the **Magistrates' Court** by Bryan Gibson

The second edition of this highly successful work explains the magistrates' court in 12 easy to read chapters. Contains a unique *Glossary of Words, Phrases and Abbreviations* with 750 entries. ISBN 1 872 870 15 5. £10

Introduction to the **Probation Service** by Anthony Osler

An outline of the work of the Probation Service, including historical background and a wide-ranging description of present day responsibilities. ISBN 1 872 870 19 8. £10

The **Interpreters Handbook** by Ruth Morris and Joan Colin

Including an introduction to the work of the court interpreter, this book also looks at the wider implications of the subject. ISBN 1 872 870 28 7. £12 (Available from Autumn 1995 onwards).

The **Sentence of the Court** A Handbook for Magistrates by Michael Watkins, Winston Gordon and Anthony Jeffries. Consultant Dr David Thomas.

An easy to read introduction to basic sentencing principles which avoids jargon and complexity. Produced under the auspices of the Justices' Clerks' Society. ISBN 1 872 870 25 2. £10 (Available from Autumn 1995 onwards)

The direct mail price of each title is given above. Please add £1.50 per volume p&p to a maximum of £6 (UK only. Postage abroad is charged at cost). Please send your order to WATERSIDE PRESS, Domum Road, Winchester S023 9NN. Telephone or Fax 01962 855567. Cheques should be made out to 'Waterside Press'. Organizations can be invoiced for two or more books on request.

THE WATERSIDE PRESS

Criminal Policy Series

An important library series for criminal justice practitioners, academics, researchers and students

Series editor Professor Andrew Rutherford

The first four titles in this series are scheduled for publication in March 1996 as follows:

THE SCOTTISH CRIMINAL JUSTICE PROCESS
Peter Young   ISBN 1 872 870 34 1

TRANSFORMING CRIMINAL POLICY
Andrew Rutherford   ISBN 1 872 870 31 7

CAPITAL PUNISHMENT: GLOBAL DEVELOPMENTS AND PROSPECTS
Peter Hodgkinson
AndrewRutherford   ISBN 1 872 870 32 5

DRUGS AND CRIMINAL JUSTICE POLICY
Penny Green   ISBN 1 872 870 33 3

Price £18 per volume plus £1.50 p&p (£60 inclusive for all four books). Prices quoted are for the UK only. Postage abroad is charged at cost.

Please send your order to WATERSIDE PRESS, Domum Road, Winchester S023 9NN. Telephone or Fax 01962 855567. Cheques should be made out to 'Waterside Press'. Organizations can be invoiced for two or more books on request.